Lavery Library

St. John Fisher
College
Rochester, New York

The Moral Advantage

Other Books by William Damon

Noble Purpose: The Joy of Living a Meaningful Life (2003)

Bringing in a New Era in Character Education (2002)

Good Work: When Excellence and Ethics Meet (2001) (with Howard Gardner and Mihaly Csikszentmihalyi)

The Youth Charter: How Communities Can Work Together to Raise Standards for All Our Children (1997)

Greater Expectations: Overcoming the Culture of Indulgence in America's Homes and Schools (1995)

Some Do Care: Contemporary Lives of Moral Commitment (1992) (with Anne Colby)

The Moral Child: Nurturing Children's Natural Moral Growth (1990)

Self-Understanding in Childhood and Adolescence (1988) (with Daniel Hart)

Social and Personality Development: Infancy through Adolescence (1983)

The Social World of the Child (1977)

The Moral Advantage

How to Succeed
in Business
by Doing
the Right Thing

WILLIAM DAMON

BK

BERRETT-KOEHLER PUBLISHERS, INC.
San Francisco

Photograph of Dame Anita Roddick on page 76 taken by Brian Moody.

Photograph of Mike Markkula on page 93 taken by Charles Barry for Santa Clara University.

Berrett-Koehler Publishers, Inc.
235 Montgomery Street, Suite 650
San Francisco, CA 94104-2916
Tel: (415) 288-0260 Fax: (415) 362-2512
www.bkconnection.com

ORDERING INFORMATION

QUANTITY SALES. Special discounts are available on quantity purchases by corporations, associations, and others. For details, contact the "Special Sales Department" at the Berrett-Koehler address above.
INDIVIDUAL SALES. Berrett-Koehler publications are available through most bookstores. They can also be ordered direct from Berrett-Koehler: Tel: (800) 929-2929; Fax: (802) 864-7626; www.bkconnection.com.
ORDERS FOR COLLEGE TEXTBOOK/COURSE ADOPTION USE. Please contact Berrett-Koehler: Tel: (800) 929-2929; Fax: (802) 864-7626.
ORDERS BY U.S. TRADE BOOKSTORES AND WHOLESALERS. Please contact Publishers Group West, 1700 Fourth Street, Berkeley, CA 94710. Tel: (510) 528-1444; Fax: (510) 528-3444.

Berrett-Koehler and the BK logo are registered trademarks of Berrett-Koehler Publishers, Inc.

Printed in the United States of America

Berrett-Koehler books are printed on long-lasting acid-free paper. When it is available, we choose paper that has been manufactured by environmentally responsible processes. These may include using trees grown in sustainable forests, incorporating recycled paper, minimizing chlorine in bleaching, or recycling the energy produced at the paper mill.

Library of Congress Cataloging-in-Publication Data

Damon, William, 1944
    The moral advantage : how to succeed in business by doing the right thing / by William Damon
        p. cm.
    Includes bibliographical references and index.
    Contents: Introduction: Purpose and success in business—The moral advantage—Generative morality:
        Acts of creation—Empathic morality and the Golden Rule—Business ethics that come naturally—
        Philanthropy in business: Doing it right—Forging a moral identity in business.
    ISBN 1-57675-206-2
        1. Business ethics. 2. Success in business—Moral and ethical aspects. 3. Social responsibility of busi-
    ness. 4. Industrial management—Moral and ethical aspects. 5. Organizational behavior—Moral and
    ethical aspects. 6. Businesspeople—Interviews. 7. Successful people. I. Title: How to succeed in busi-
    ness by doing the right thing. II. Title.
    HF5387.D26   2004
    174'.5—dc22   2004041147

Project Manager: Katherine Silver, BookMatters; *Copyeditor:* Amy Smith Bell; *Proofreader:* Mike Mollett; *Designer/Compositor:* Bea Hartman, BookMatters; *Indexer:* Ken DellaPenta
09   08   07   06   05   04
10   9   8   7   6   5   4   3   2   1

*To Sir John Templeton,
visionary businessman and philanthropist*

Contents

Preface

This book describes what I consider to be the most rewarding pathways to success and satisfaction in a business career. I have drawn my conclusions from extensive interviews with men and women who have forged extraordinary business careers while focusing on their loftiest purposes and deepest convictions. Readers who are hoping to thrive in the business world will find useful guidance in the examples set by these men and women.

I could have used such guidance early in my own life. When I was young, I got two different kinds of career advice, pretty much at odds with one another. The first was idealistic: Aim high, do what you believe in (or what you love, mostly amounting to the same thing), always act in ways that you'll be proud of, and so on. The second kind was gritty and more "realistic," sometimes to the point of cynicism: nice guys finish last; you need to go along to get along; don't bite the hand that feeds you; remember what side of your bread the butter is on; if you want to really make it, you'll need to have sharp elbows and maybe be a bit of a thief. Memorable as they were to me, these conflicting maxims indicate the confusion that many young people feel when thinking about the "right" way to orient their careers. Nor does the confusion end by midcareer. Most ambitious people continue to look for the most fruitful directions to take throughout their entire working life, and many never stop feeling conflicts between their highest aspirations and the temptation to compromise those aspirations for the sake of survival and success.

This book describes a way of doing business that makes such conflicts and confusion unnecessary. The mode of doing business that I describe is highly successful, yet it requires no trade-offs of principle or conviction. Rather, men and women who operate in this manner gain their competitive edge by strategically employing their convictions. I call this edge "the moral advantage."

At a time when many people in business have become convinced that the road to success is paved with compromise, this message is urgent and necessary. Few people ever *want* to compromise their principles or standards: they do so because they believe they must. When they do, they compromise gradually, chipping away bit by bit at the dreams they had when they first decided on their life's work. And before long, like the doomed frog in a pot of water that heats up one degree at a time, their dreams gradually expire.

If selling out our deepest beliefs and principles were truly necessary for success, we might need to recognize that and somehow come to terms with it. But what if it is not only unnecessary but counterproductive? What if staying true to your highest purposes and convictions actually offers the surest route to the most satisfying and rewarding kind of success? I make that case here, and I chart this direction for those who have the courage to take this route.

One clarification at the outset: I do not mean by "the moral advantage" that those who act morally necessarily make the most money. If we create a two-by-two contingency table laying out all the possibilities, each box would have cases in it: crooks who makes lots of money, crooks who make little or no money, moral people who make little or no money, and moral people who make lots of money. All of these possibilities do in fact happen in the real world.

In this book, I am only interested in the fourth possibility— moral people who succeed—and even here, my interest goes beyond moneymaking per se. My interest, really, is in how people succeed in the broadest possible sense: how they can achieve their financial goals, build satisfying and enduring careers, make a positive difference in the world, and feel proud of the work they do and its contribution to society. All people, if they think that they have the choice, want this kind of total success. And of this I am sure: only people who take a moral approach, staying true to their convictions and highest aspirations, have careers that are fulfilling in every sense of the word. The examples that I have assembled in this book offer evidence that people in business do have this choice.

From 1998 to 2003, in collaboration with my colleagues Mihaly Csikszentmihalyi and Howard Gardner and our research teams at Stanford University, Harvard University, the University of Chicago, and the Claremont Graduate University, I interviewed forty-eight men and women who have had, or are having, success in the business world. Many of these men and women were founders or heads of large companies, others are leading smaller companies, and others still are now climbing up the corporate ladder or growing their own businesses. These business leaders have demonstrated excellence in entrepreneurial or managerial skills, and this excellence has been rewarded with recognition and financial success. As I demonstrate in this book, the mastery of business skills that these leaders have shown has been sustained by a sense of moral purpose and high ethical standards, and these have been key elements in their continued achievement and life satisfaction.

Throughout the book, I quote from many of the interviews that my colleagues and I conducted as a way of bringing life to my points. When I do so, I identify the subject with the position that he or she held at the time of the interview, or in a few cases, with the position that he or she held when experiencing the event referred to in the quotation. Because the business world is fluid, and because lives of busy people change, I am sure that many, if not most, of these interviewees will have moved on to other challenges by the time this book is published.

I began this project when CEOs were still held high in public esteem, seemingly a lifetime ago. By the time my research was completed, in early 2004, *moral* may indeed have become the last word

in the English language that the public uses to describe its contemporary business leaders. Yet in the careers of the men and
women whom I interviewed, I found a vast amount of "good
work"—that is, work that is both excellent and ethical. One of my
colleagues, Csikszentmihalyi, has written about how people in
business, including some in our study, can use processes such as
"flow" (Csikszentmihalyi's own widely known term for optimal
motivation) to accomplish their good work.[1] Another colleague,
Gardner, has written about the cognitive processes that leaders in
business and other fields use to change directions when good work
requires it.[2] My focus is how successful businesspeople use their
convictions to build careers marked with distinction. My own conviction is that all men and women in business, whatever their age
or status, can use these same moral strategies to put their careers on
track for success and personal satisfaction.

In this book, I identify the key strategies of a moral approach to
business and show exactly how these strategies can be used to promote personal and professional success. I examine the moral center
of business in a more complete—and a more positive—manner
than the standard "business ethics" approach that has been prevalent
in business schools and corporate training seminars. I draw this contrast in Chapter 5. For now, I simply note that the compelling examples of the men and women whom I have interviewed made it easy
for me to emphasize the positive as well as the prudential contributions of the moral advantage.

Whenever I use the word *moral* in my writings, some readers
naturally ask me what I mean—or, to put it another way, to whose
morality am I referring? I mean nothing fancy or controversial by
the word; I am simply referring to the morality shared by people of
goodwill everywhere. This includes aspirations to make the world a
better place, to act decently, to care for one's family and one's neighbors, to live honorably, and to be kind, fair, honest, and responsible.
As I have discussed in detail in my other books, these aspirations are
lifelong and universal: even young children feel the tugs of empathy,
compassion, and social obligation, and people all over the world
resonate toward similar moral urges.[3] To be sure, there are con-

tentious issues that divide people, but when it comes to the core moral goals and codes of human conduct, there is a broad consensus among all the world's great religions and civilized social orders. I draw on this widespread consensus whenever I write about moral commitment.

My study of the moral route to business success originally grew out of a broader exploration of how it is possible for any professional to acquire moral integrity and excel in one's work during times when the strongest incentives seem to be pushing him or her in the other direction. With my colleagues Gardner and Csikszentmihalyi, I have examined such good work in several professional fields, and two years ago we wrote an initial book on the topic, focusing on good work in science and journalism.[4] The present book on morally based success in business is the next step in my efforts to identify the pathways to leading a career that is both satisfying to the individual who pursues it and essential to the society that supports such careers.

Good work means work that is both successful and responsible, both masterful and moral. Too often in today's world, ambitious people feel pressured to cut corners or give up their loftiest goals to get ahead. But good work resists such compromises. It has a moral center. It always aims to fulfill a noble purpose. People who do the best work hold onto all their dreams and standards, knowing that this is the surest way to achieve real and lasting success.

□   □   □

Many individuals and funding agencies have supported the Good Work Project and its present extension into the business arena. First and foremost, the John Templeton Foundation supported the business study from which the main conclusions in this book are drawn. I would like to thank Arthur Schwartz of that foundation for his most gracious and helpful feedback on my work over the years. The William and Flora Hewlett Foundation was the original major funder of the broader Good Work Project, beginning with the domains of journalism and science. The Hewlett Foundation has continued to support the project generously, especially with respect to the area of philanthropy, and I would like to thank its president, Paul Brest, for his help, advice, and interest. In addition, the Atlantic Philanthropies has funded the philanthropy study generously, and I would like especially to thank Joel Fleishman for his gracious support. I discuss findings from our philanthropy research in Chapter 6. The Carnegie Corporation of New York and the Ford Foundation also have given the Good Work Project much appreciated support.

I also offer special thanks to the King family and their Thrive Foundation for generous support of my research as well as for many stimulating conversations and spiritual guidance. In a similar vein, I wish to thank Courtney Ross Holst for her early support of the Good Work Project through the Ross Family Foundation and for support of many other kinds, including a most welcome stay at the Ross Institute on Long Island, New York, where I had the opportunity to finish this manuscript.

An early version of sections of Chapter 2 was published in *Optimize* magazine in January 2002. Although I have since reformulated many of the notions that I expressed in that article, I appreciated the opportunity to try out some ideas that I was developing in that vigorous publication. At Stanford, my research assistants Barbara Wang Tolentino, Mollie Galloway, and Peter Osborn contributed greatly to the interviews and analyses reported in this book. Susan Verducci and Liza Hayes Percer helped with the analyses and offered highly intelligent feedback, and Tanya Rose, Kathy Davis, and Taru Fisher also provided invaluable support. I thank the staffs of my colleagues at Harvard, the University of Chicago, and the Claremont Graduate University for their assistance in the interview process and for many useful discussions about the project's results.

January 2004
Mattapoisett, Massachusetts

Introduction: Success and Satisfaction in Business

Some time ago, I gave a lecture to a group of students who had just entered a teacher-training program. In the group, there was the usual smattering of recent college graduates eager to get started on a teaching career. But there were a number of more wizened faces as well, slightly older people in their thirties and forties who were preparing for their first job in a classroom. Where, I wondered, had they come from? What had brought them to this place, after what must have been some serious attempts at first trying something else?

After the lecture, I hung around to chat. Soon I found out that some of the older students had dropped out of law or medicine, a couple had been in the military, but by far the greatest number had just left careers in business. Had they failed? In many cases, no, at least not in the material sense. Some had been in secure jobs, others said they had been on fast tracks in the corporate world, and still others had run franchises or even started their own profitable enterprises.

What none of these folks professed to have was a sense that they had been accomplishing things that really mattered to them, or even that something of consequence happened when they went to work each day. They were neither especially proud of the work that they were doing nor of the kinds of workers that they had become. For some of these people, this meant a nagging discomfort about the cutthroat acts and semi-shady dealings that they had felt called on to carry out. For others, it was more a depressing sense that they were wasting their time on goals that reflected neither their own deepest concerns nor those of anyone else. These men and women had come to the teaching profession with the expectation that here, at least, they could make a difference in the futures of young people.

I am sure that there are dozens of other fields that attract refugees from the business world. Some people will find the sense of meaningful calling that they had failed to find in business, and others no doubt will continue to drift. Business is by no means the only field in which workers have a hard time finding personal meaning these days.

We are not always aware of the forces that ultimately move us. While focusing on "how" questions—how to survive, how to get ahead, how to make a name for ourselves—often we forget the "why" questions that are more essential for finding and staying on the best course: Why pursue this objective? Why behave in this manner? Why aspire to this kind of life? Why become this kind of person?

These "why" questions help us realize our highest aspirations and our truest interests. To answer these questions well, we must decide what matters most to us, what we will be able to contribute to in our careers, what are the right (as opposed to the wrong) ways of behaving as we aim toward this end, and, ultimately, what kind of persons we want to be. Because everyone, everywhere, wants to live an admirable life, a life of consequence, the "why" questions cannot be ignored for long without great peril to one's personal stability and enduring success. It is like ignoring the rudder on a ship—no matter how much you look after all the boat's other moving parts, you may end up lost at sea.

In a vague and uncertain way, many people in business realize this. But they do not always know how to act on it. In fact, many have the mistaken belief that too much attention to their deepest purposes and convictions may get in the way of their career goals. They consider their higher aspirations to be often in opposition to the real path to business success. To survive in business, they feel that they need to put their moral values on hold. They may feel forced to trade off their sense of right and wrong, their sense of moral purpose, against their material ambitions. This is not a trade-off that leaves anyone comfortable. Rather, it leaves people feeling co-opted, hijacked away from the places where they were when they started out, a place where they had expected to stay.

Adding to this feeling is the instability of the times, an age of blinding change, with everything from fierce international forces to revolutionary new technologies altering the economic conditions of business daily. Periods of rapid change always escalate the pressure on individuals to abandon their personal moorings. Adapting to a new, often bewildering set of conditions requires so much attention that people may be hard-pressed to keep in mind their most basic orienting principles. Change demands flexibility, a giving up of old ways. It is never easy to decide which of the "old ways" are essential to the very core of one's identity and sense of purpose, so essential that they can never be given up, whatever the risk. Caught in the midst of this fog, workers struggle to find the right direction, and too often, in a state of quiet panic, they throw overboard the very instruments they need to give them their bearings.

Many people in business today feel lost or "misplaced." In the normal course of events, however, they rarely articulate this feeling, even to themselves. It is not a happy condition, yet determined workers can manage the discomfort and stay in this state of being indefinitely. Sometimes, though, a crisis yanks them out of this state involuntarily. "Improprieties" are discovered, a company implodes, a reputation is shattered. No matter that the "improprieties" had once been considered routine ways of doing business—someone *else* is now asking the "why" questions that had been too long ignored. Or, in a less dramatic but still distressing turn of events, a company or a worker runs out of steam and becomes devoid of the strategies, effective ideas, and the focus needed to come back.

It does not need to be this way. There are many chances to do good work in business without compromising your deepest convictions. There are many examples of successful men and women in business who have done so. They draw on all their best values and

aspirations as they pursue their career goals. This unity of purpose—
a combination of the desires to excel, to accomplish something
important, and to act in a decent and responsible way—is characteristic of many successful business leaders, the men and women
who have risen to the top and stayed there, year after year.

How to develop this unity of purpose and enduring focus—
what I call "the moral advantage"—is the subject of this book. To
provide living examples of how this is done, I draw on cases of forty-
eight business leaders whom my colleagues and I interviewed for our
study of "good work."[1] As a way of setting an illuminating contrast,
I also note a case or two in which the moral advantage was sorely
lacking, an experience I know firsthand from a youthful misadven-
ture in my own high-school years.

Why do people go into business to begin with? Although we
each may have our own particular reasons, the most general answer
is "to make a lot of money"—an answer that is true enough as far as
it goes. Moneymaking is an essential aim, a necessary condition, an
index of success, a desired prize, the most sought-after "coin of the
realm" for anyone in business. Without monetary gain, or at least
the anticipation of it, a life in business is not much of a life.

But this obvious answer, when taken out of context, can be misleading. Indeed it *has* been misleading for too many people, especially those struggling to get their bearings in a field rife with obses-
sions about the fiscal bottom line. There is nothing more futile than
a narrow, tunnel-vision devotion to financial gain as a lone goal.
Although everyone who goes into business naturally wants to make
plenty of money, those who are destined to succeed in the most satisfying ways go into business with dreams of accomplishment that
are far more interesting—and rewarding—than monetary gain for
its own sake.

As a business career plays out, for better or for worse, in most
cases money ends up being just one part of the story—and usually
not the most memorable part. Some people who single-mindedly
attempt to achieve financial success without keeping in touch with
their other goals and values burn out, fail, or eke out mediocre
careers in insignificant corners of the business world. Those who do

manage to achieve financial success without satisfying their other aspirations often end up feeling barren and dispirited. Those who truly thrive year in and year out, building enduring careers that provide them with recognition in their work and meaning in their personal lives, keep a bottom line of a different sort in mind while they pursue their financial goals.

As a life-span developmental psychologist, I have met hundreds of people who have left, or are longing to leave, their business careers to enter other vocational paths. Some leave after records of success and financial reward, some leave broke and feeling beaten up. Others leave their professions because they couldn't stand the pressure, still others because they didn't like their positions on the corporate ladder, or because they found the work boring or meaningless, or because they hoped to find a more fulfilling or personally rewarding vocation. Each story of longing and departure looks different from all the others, and each has its own unique pattern of reasons and regrets.

Underlying all the variety, I have noticed one thing that many of these stories have in common: *People leaving business careers often complain that they were forced to give up the values and purposes that led them to choose business in the first place.* In other words, they felt that they had drifted away from their initial, fundamental moorings and they did not like where they were ending up.

More than a dozen years ago, my wife and coauthor Anne Colby and I examined the lives of another twenty-three Americans—not, for the most part, businesspeople, although there were three or four in the group who fitted that bill.[2] What the twenty-three had in common was that they all had dedicated their lives to charitable service and other altruistic causes. The work that they were doing was hard and risky, often without apparent reward. I knew that we would find these people admirable in many ways, but before our study I had little sense of how appreciative they themselves were of their own chosen paths. In fact, I rather expected to find this group conducting their lives with a kind of grim fortitude, constantly fending off despair and gearing up their courage.

It turned out that nothing could be further from the truth. The joy and positivity that these extraordinary men and women expressed about their opportunities to serve was astonishing. They each denied that they ever had demonstrated self-sacrifice, fortitude, or courage. Rather, they said their actions felt so automatic and involuntary that they never questioned or doubted their work, and that they rarely worried about dangers or other adverse personal consequences. For example, Suzie Valadez, a lifelong missionary, said her work felt as natural as moving out of the way of a speeding bus. She had relocated from California to Ciudad Juarez for forty years in order to bring schooling and medical care to Mexican families who had been scraping out an existence on the edge of a garbage dump. In other words, there was no sense of trade-off in the choices that our twenty-three exemplars made. They did not feel that they were sacrificing something by committing themselves to good work. They were doing what they wanted to do, and they felt as fulfilled as any people we have known in our own personal or professional lives.

That study stayed with me intellectually and emotionally long after its completion, in part because of its message that some people find ways to do enormous good in the world without becoming martyrs, silent sufferers, or good-natured victims. Admittedly, these people were unusual. But the more I thought about it, the more I became convinced that such people travel in many circles, not only among the ranks of those whose life work is dedicated to wholly altruistic causes such as charitable service. In industry, in the arts, in the professions, I could think of many renowned people who approach their work in such a manner: accepting no trade-offs between ambition and integrity, between success and purpose.

At that point I had a strange thought, strange not because of its oddity but because of its violation of our conventional cynicism: *Perhaps certain kinds of success—the most significant and enduring kinds—actually depend on a determination to accept no compromises or trade-offs in our moral convictions.* That is, perhaps the moral road is the surest path to both success *and* fulfillment. Perhaps for all of us, it is wisest to aim for alignment between our moral and personal goals rather than calculating how much and how often we should pay tribute to the moral versus the personal.

Of course this is not the usual way of thinking about the relation between business and morality. Observers of business usually assume that people at the top must put their moral values on hold to get ahead. Competitive achievement is often viewed as morally compromised to begin with. Enterprise for profit is seen as fundamentally self-serving. Good work, it is assumed, can only be done at the margins, on the sly, or after one has made one's bundle. Those who have made the case for capitalism's moral core—Adam Smith in the eighteenth century, Frederick Hayek and Joseph Schumpeter in the mid-twentieth century, Thomas Sowell and Michael Novak more recently—often have been considered little more than apologists for the powerful and wealthy.

But how do those in the arena actually see it? How do businesspeople, especially the "captains of industry" considered by many to be morally suspect, orient to their work? Do they approach their moral obligation as an unwelcome nuisance, a public relations chore, a constraint that they wish they could do away with? Or might their sense of moral purpose be at the heart of their achievements and success?

After examining the lives and careers of the business leaders profiled in this book, I can write with confidence that many of them operate out of a sense of purpose, often moral in tone, and a commitment to conduct themselves in an ethical way. Their personal ambitions, their aspirations to contribute something important to the world, and their personal values are thoroughly intertwined, in many cases inseparable. These leaders draw creativity and staying power from their senses of purpose, and they subject themselves to the discipline imposed by their commitment to ethical standards.

The message of this book is that *anyone* can operate in this way—a way that, sooner or later, will bestow a moral advantage on both one's career and one's search for personal fulfillment. This does not always come easily, especially under conditions of financial pressure and rapid change. But many of these leaders have learned how to function in this way, often by looking at the example of those who have found ways to do so in other challenging circumstances.

I will never forget a realization I had when examining the question of how some journalists manage to do good work despite the deterioration of the overall conditions in the media industry. From national news anchors to cub reporters in an obscure country town, some of the country's best reporters keep the same portrait over their desks: the determined visage of Edward R. Murrow, an icon of journalistic excellence and integrity. Many reporters look to that picture whenever they have a moment of doubt about what to do next. What would Murrow do? This is also the way they keep in touch with their own convictions. By acting in the manner of a revered exemplar, they can pass their own "mirror test": they like what they see in their own reflections.

All businesspeople can benefit from the instructive and inspiring examples of those who use moral means to achieve enduring success. But in the business community at large there are not many widely revered icons such as Ed Murrow. Nor have all people in business had the benefit of real-life mentors who exemplify admirable qualities. As a consequence, many businessmen and -women often come up empty-handed when they search for guidance on this front. This book intends to fill that need.

The notion that moral purpose can play an important role is not new. What *is* new here is a detailed account of the various and particular ways in which this works, beginning with the generative role that moral purpose can play. As I show throughout the book, a sense of moral purpose can be a fertile source of innovation in business. It can be a wellspring of creative inspiration, not merely a restraint on illegitimate behavior. This is not the kind of moral awareness that you will read about in many business ethics courses—which, of course, is why so few students pay attention to their business-school ethics requirements. As I formulate it in this book, the moral advantage is a positive way of thinking about morality that transforms both the worker and the work, a powerful force that can propel people toward their own goals while at the same time generating great benefits for society.

Three Assumptions about Everyday Morality

I begin this book with three assumptions, each of which is solidly grounded in philosophy and the social sciences. Yet they are not well understood by many of the "experts" who speak and write about business ethics, resulting in lots of unnecessary confusion about how morality works in everyday business dealings.

1. Most people (with the exception of the pure saints or sinners found in fairytales and other fables) approach their life choices with mixed motives. That is to say, in the normal course of events, human motives tend to be in part altruistic and in part self-serving. Most accomplishments are spurred by mixed motives. To do good work, we do not need to forgo our own self-oriented needs; but we do need to keep our moral voices alive and active, especially when encountering hard-to-resist pressures and temptations.

2. Morality is a broad and inclusive concept with a positive spirit at its center. Unlike some popular conceptions of morality, a true moral sense goes way beyond the kinds of ethical constraints that appear as "do not" rules (e.g., do not steal, do not lie, do not cheat, do not sexually harass your employees, and so on). Although ethical proscriptions may be what many think of first when they use the term *moral*, morality also includes a positive dedication to doing good, a sense of service to humanity, a commitment to a larger purpose.

3. *Moral integrity*, as the term implies, means an integration of our moral concerns with all the other components of our character, including our deepest personal inclinations. It does not require us to sacrifice ourselves entirely for the sake of our altruistic ideals. That approach leads in the end to martyrdom, which fortunately is not necessary for moral integrity (except, sadly, in extreme circumstances). But the search for moral integrity does call on us to keep our natural egotistical inclinations in perspective, through virtues such as honesty and humility. Moral integrity requires keeping in mind the moral implications of our behavior at all times, rather than cutting corners now with the thought of making up for it later.

These assumptions matter greatly, because without them it is easy to dismiss morality as an inconsequential part of life. Without awareness of the first assumption, morality can be caricatured as the province of naive idealists and losers who are not serious about getting ahead in the rough-and-tumble world. Without awareness of the second assumption, morality is reduced to a bunch of sermons and prohibitions. Without awareness of the third assumption, morality becomes little more than an after-the-fact gesture, a mathematical game to redress the damage one has done. In contrast to such sterile but all-too-common notions of morality, this book presents a view of morality that places it at the center of the good life, connected to every source of personal satisfaction and creative fulfillment. The remaining part of this Introduction addresses how these three assumptions can help people understand the role of the moral voice in business success.

□ *The Moral Voice Does Not Sing Alone:*
  Good Work Always Arises from Mixed Motives

At the most elevated levels of moral commitment, the personal and the moral become almost fused. True moral exemplars can barely distinguish between the two. In *Some Do Care,* Colby and I examined the lives and work of men and women who had been widely recognized as living moral exemplars—that is, persons whose actions had represented the finest principles and ideals in society.[3] Some of these people had devoted their lives to causes of charity, others to education, civil rights, peace, liberty, health care, justice, and so on. We found that these men and women felt that the work they were doing fulfilled both personal *and* moral goals. In fact, because of this dual fulfillment, they were able to tackle tough problems and accomplish big results year after year.

Almost all major achievements in life are fueled by motives that are in part self-serving and in part aimed at purposes larger than the self. This is true not only of achievements that appear extraordinarily altruistic but also of just plain good work. Some people, like the moral exemplars covered in *Some Do Care,* integrate their personal and moral motives so completely that they experience them as inseparable. But most people, inevitably, do distinguish between the two as they go about their lives. Most people recognize a difference between feathering their own nests and contributing something toward the welfare of others. Sometimes people are more driven by self-serving goals and other times by goals that serve the larger society. Eventually, most people try to recognize the importance of both types of goals, tackling endeavors that reflect some combination of the two.

Because most people are driven by mixed motives, does this mean that there can be no distinctions between any endeavors with regard to their moral worth? That is, if most endeavors are "tainted" with self-interest, should we treat just about anything that anyone does with equal cynicism? Not at all. There are two tried-and-true ways to determine the moral worth of any course of action:

1. Does the course of action follow moral means in pursuit of its ends?
2. If the moral course of action places at risk the self-interest of the actor, will it be pursued anyway?

The first of these moral litmus tests, the means-ends requirement, winnows out an enormous list of pretenders from those who operate with genuine integrity. Almost all people justify, to themselves and others, the moral validity of their goals. Hitler, Stalin, Idi Amin, Pol Pot—they all professed to be acting out of selfless humanitarian concerns. Partly because many people found such claims persuasive, these monstrous leaders managed to attract huge numbers of supporters. The real monstrosities were the absolutely unscrupulous means that these leaders used to pursue their goals. Deception, murder, torture—all were fair game in the name of the "noble" cause. The evil was not only in the causes (although these too were deeply flawed) but also in the abominations carried out in their names.

In more banal cases, such as politicians who deceive their constituents in order to get support for beneficial pieces of legislation, the harm done—the corrosion of trust, the weakening of the democratic system—can be slow and harder to detect, but the principle and the ultimate effects are the same. Immoral means inevitably undermine the social value of any endeavor. For this reason, it is wise and proper to admire not only those who claim to aspire to noble-sounding results but also those who restrict themselves to ethical codes of conduct in their quest.

The second litmus test—a willingness to sacrifice one's self-interest for the sake of a moral principle—is more difficult to apply directly, because in the normal course of human events, morality and self-interest often go hand in hand.[4] That, in fact, is one of the basic claims of this book. Whenever a mother nurtures her baby, whenever a child shares a toy with a friend in a game, whenever a worker chooses *not* to reach into a coworker's purse and lift her wallet, morality and self-interest are combined. In fact, the reason that such actions seem unremarkable—indeed, almost natural and automatic—is that they provoke no conflict between morality and self-interest. What is right is also what one *wants* to do, so there is no problem that requires conscious mediation. For those who are not habitual sociopaths, the bulk of normal everyday social activity—most of daily life—combines morality and self-interest in precisely this way.

Only in occasional circumstances—important ones, to be sure, but nevertheless circumstances out of the ordinary—do morality and self-interest come into opposition with one another and require making choices. By looking at a person's actions over time, it is possible to gain a sense of the person's priorities. Does the mother act warmly when the baby is pleasing her but turn a cold shoulder when the baby is unresponsive, difficult, or needy? Does a child share readily when he feels like playing and then turn stingy when he gets bored with the game or the other players? Does the worker resist blatantly ripping off colleagues but find other ways to take advantage of them when she can get away with it? In each of these cases, the person's moral feelings are submerged when the interests of the self are not wholly aligned with those of the other. This reveals that the moral part of the person's mixed motives do not assume a very high priority in the mix.

□ *The Rarely Recognized Moral Part*
   of Mixed Motives in Business

Mixed motives are as much the rule in business as in any other domain in life. Prominent in business are self-promotional goals such as moneymaking, status-seeking, power-grabbing, and personal ego-boosting. At the same time, many people in business—not all, but many—also pursue goals that promote the interests of others, such as serving customers well, producing goods that the world needs or wants, treating employees fairly, building companies that they can pass on to the next generation, and improving communities. Almost every business career that is successful over the long run reflects some such mix of aspirations to serve self and others.

Typically, when thinking about what drives businesspeople, the nobler part of the mix gets shorter shrift than the self-serving part. When noble motives in business are acknowledged at all, they are generally considered to be little more than grudging concessions to social reality, perhaps for the sake of public relations, perhaps simply to stay out of trouble. The effort to act responsibly in business is often viewed as an imposed burden that businesspeople must put up with, certainly not of their own free will.

Indeed, skeptical attitudes toward the motives of people in business date back to ancient times; and by the twentieth century, the skepticism had become dominant in much of Western culture. To be sure, there have been influential religious leaders who have taken a different tack, portraying business as a "calling" meant to serve God. But most of those voices are silent now, and the notion of business as a faith-inspired calling has long since faded in the public mind.[5] Within the academy, the press, the nonprofit sector, and the entertainment industry, the consensus is that people in business are driven mainly by greed. And because greed is seen as the primary motive, it is generally assumed that people in business will take the low road to success whenever they can get away with it.

Now there is no question that money, and lots of it, can be made on the low road, through fraud, brazen chicanery, shameless hype, reckless gambling, and irresponsible plundering. The annals of business are full of take-the-money-and-run schemes that have rewarded fast deals, lucrative tricks, lucky bets, wild hits, and get-rich-quick ploys that have left companies and the employees, investors, customers, and communities that supported them in shambles. Such stories are well-known; they make for good reading, and the press glories in reporting them. The most notorious cases end up in criminal or civil court, with blaring media exposure. Many people who operate this way—the lion's share, perhaps—manage to keep low profiles while hoarding their ill-gotten gains.

Yet even the bitterest critics of capitalism would admit that there are higher roads to business success than this. Plenty of money can be made by dealing honestly, by producing genuinely needed goods and services, by fair dealing, and by responsible conduct. No one can deny that there are successful business leaders who treat their customers well, who act respectfully toward their employees, and who care about their communities. How prevalent such cases are might be argued, but there is little question that many exist.

In this book, I make the case that the high roads to business success are more traveled than today's conventional wisdom would tell us. This is not to say that those who take the high road do so with purely altruistic motives, or that they behave in saintly manners throughout their careers. Indeed, these actors are as personally ambitious as any other aspiring businessperson, and they may pursue egoistic and materialistic goals. But higher motives drive these people too, motives that derive from their senses of right and wrong, from their desires to contribute to the world, from their feelings of obligation, from the call of service. Such moral concerns are an inextricable part of the motivational mix that fuels their energies.

□ *Morality Is a Positive Force in Human Life,*
  Not Just a Set of Stifling Constraints

When I began studying moral development more than twenty-five years ago, the prevalent view in the social sciences was that morality arose from fear of punishment, power, and negative feelings such as shame and guilt—which are simply one's own way of punishing the self psychologically. My early studies on the origins of morality found a different set of motives. I discovered that young children share toys with friends because they think it is fair, and also because they like their friends and want to see them happy. I came up with evidence showing that these positive moral inclinations—denoted "fairness" and "empathy" in their full-blown guises—could be found in essentially all children.[6] What's more, children stick by these moral inclinations even in the face of adult injunctions to the contrary (that is, kids will share with friends even if Mom or Dad says not to). So much for power and punishment as morality's primary source. As I moved up the life span, I found many other examples of positive morality: choices shaped by idealism and noble purpose in adolescence;[7] a sense of work as a moral calling among leading professionals;[8] and the joys of moral commitment among persons who had dedicated their lives to transcendent causes.[9]

Within the scientific field of human development, I believe that it is fair to say that the positive role of morality in human affairs is now firmly established. Almost all modern textbooks now reflect this view. At the same time, a fortuitous shift in the fields of social and personality psychology, led by Martin Seligman and Mihaly Csikszentmihalyi, has opened the doors of the broader discipline's perception to proactive as well as reactive sources of human motivation.[10] These "positive psychologists" reject the idea that people's goals and values arise from basic drives such as hunger and sex (as the behaviorists once believed), or from defense mechanisms such as sublimation and reaction formation (as the Freudians once believed). Rather, they believe that people can and do freely choose goals and values that promote such higher purposes as morality, creativity, and spirituality. Leaders of the positive psychology movement use notions such as "authentic happiness" (Seligman), "optimal experience" (Csikszentmihalyi), and "ultimate concerns" (Robert Emmons) to capture the essence of our most lofty and enlightened desires.[11] Moral purpose and moral inspiration are now officially on the radar screen of today's social sciences.

The idea that morality plays an essential role in business—or at least that it ought to—is by no means unique to this book (although, as recent headlines have made clear, it is an idea more voiced than followed). What may be unique is this book's determinedly positive account of the moral approach that underlies a successful career, beginning with the *creative* and *generative* insights that I describe in Chapter 3 and continuing with the interpersonal, ethical, and philanthropic uses of moral insight that I discuss in Chapters 4, 5, and 6. As I show, a positive sense of moral purpose is a fertile source of innovative ideas and productive relations in business.

□   *The Search for Moral Integrity Requires a Dedication
     to Honesty and Humility at All Times, and Not Merely
     as a Matter of Future Intent*

In all phases of a career—the years of preparation, the years of productivity, the final years of consolidation—there can be no substi-
tute for integrity. Moral integrity means, quite literally, an integration of virtue throughout one's conduct at all times. A person with
integrity can be counted on to remain true to *all* the goals, purposes,
and standards that he or she believes in, rather than selling out one
in favor of another.

Moral integrity in business has many faces. It can assert itself
with a simple and truthful "I don't know" when an investor
demands a number prematurely, or when a boss asks for an answer
that you don't have. Integrity comes into play whenever you feel
pressured to abandon the goals that you believe in, or tempted to
stop trying to do the work that you entered the field to accomplish:
for example, when a news manager programs sensationalistic
schlock rather than important news out of fear of losing ratings, or
when a tire manufacturer allows dangerous defects to slip through in
order to undercut a competitor's prices.

The public side of integrity is *honesty*. The truth will come out
eventually, and reputations are built on the basis of credibility or
deceit. The private side of integrity is *humility*, the willingness to
admit your own imperfections, to self-correct, change course, and
keep growing. These two h's—honesty and humility—are central to
good work in business. It is hard for a person who is dishonest and
arrogant to learn from failure; and it is hard for a person who is both
honest and humble to do much harm in the long run.

The Philanthropic Solution

Some believe that a way to salvage virtue in business is by taking a
seemingly magnanimous tack: "Make your money first, any way
you can, then concentrate on using it to do some good. Grab success
by whatever means necessary—you can always redeem yourself later

through good works." What about this commonly tread path of waiting until later to contribute to society through charitable acts? Many well-intentioned people in business turn eagerly to this solution, because they do indeed want to make a difference, to leave something worthwhile behind, to feel that their material gain has done some good beyond just making themselves a bundle. So they figure that they will settle the score by giving back some of that bundle to others philanthropically. This is a familiar way to try to "have it all"—a feathered nest and a sense of moral well-being.

But there are real problems with the solution of philanthropy as a sole means to a moral sense of purpose in business. As preachers often remind their flock, sinners who wait until the eve of judgment day to reform their acts too often never get there. Life has a way of disrupting such plans—through sudden disappointments, unanticipated temptations, twists of fate, or premature death. More problematic still, an act of philanthropy, no matter how generous, cannot undo the damage caused by a wholly self-serving business career. I refer here not only to damage done to society—cheating customers, impoverishing investors, wrecking the community, and so on—but also to oneself, by denying in the prime of life that essential, fulfilling sense that one is engaged in good work.

Most troubling, philanthropy is an endeavor that can go terribly awry if it is done in the wrong way. Giving money away does not ensure a socially useful outcome. In fact, misdirected philanthropy actually does more harm than good. The right way to do philanthropy is with the same convictions that make for a moral life in business. People who in their work lives have not cultivated moral purposes nor developed virtues such as honesty and humility will be unprepared to do good philanthropy late in life, no matter how rich their financial balance sheets. I realize that this may seem a surprising notion, so I have devoted Chapter 6 to showing why and how this is so. That chapter is meant as a cautionary tale for the legions of wealthy businesspeople who make the common mistake of looking for salvation late in life by transforming themselves into philanthropists.

□   *Moral Purpose and Success Go Hand in Hand*

I can hear full well, ringing in my ears, the objections to the idea
that purpose and success in business must be pursued *together,* as a
piece; that they must not be separated; that they do not stand in
opposition to one another; that they need not be traded off against
one another in the course of a career. "This is just idealistic non-
sense," some may object. "You get ahead in business by keeping
your eye on the ball, attending to the bottom line, squeezing the
most out of every chance to cash in, letting nothing stand in your
way. Getting distracted by high-minded dreams and noble purposes
is a loser's game. If you're looking for meaning, read a book or go to
church."

Yet when a person keeps both purpose and success in mind, the
two goals promote one another. When a person separates these two,
or allows one to fall by the wayside, the person places at risk *all* the
aspirations, personal and moral, that he or she holds. There are
many reasons for preventing these two goals from becoming
detached. On the positive side, the integration of purpose and success opens the way to insights that lead to better work and competitive advantages. On the negative side, their separation leads to risks
that can derail any career.

All business success means the creation of wealth, which en-
riches founders and shareholders. But *enduring* and *personally satisfying* business success means providing something of worth to customers, supporting employees, serving the public interest, and
making a contribution to the world. It means not only accumulat-
ing money for oneself, but also building a beneficial enterprise that
creates value for society, that endures and thrives, and that continues to grow. For this kind of achievement, money is a means to a
larger end rather than an end in itself; and the low and the high
roads toward that end are not equally serviceable. The high road
bestows a proven advantage, a moral advantage, and it is the only
sure way to reach the destination.

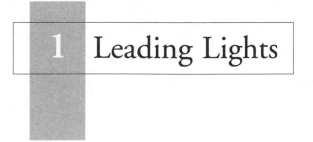

1 Leading Lights

Lars Kolind, named Denmark's Man of the Year in 1996, is one of the world's most admired businessmen. When he was in charge of Oticon Corporation, a high-quality manufacturer of hearing aids and other technologies, he helped transform the company into a knowledge-based organization in which new ideas could be generated and tested without being blocked by the kind of bureaucratic hurdles that are common in large corporations. Within seven years after taking the company public, Kolind increased its market value by a factor of fifty. After leaving Oticon, he founded his own business discovery fund (PreVenture A/S), served on several boards of multinational corporations, and started The Copenhagen Centre, a government agency that fosters partnerships between the public and private sectors.

I reached Kolind by telephone in Copenhagen. Earlier that same week, I had noticed his picture on the cover of a prominent weekly Danish magazine. Kolind's celebrity status in Denmark is a result of the "spaghetti organization" concept that he defined and promoted as Oticon CEO and board member. (During our interview, he half-complained to me about being known as "the spaghetti man"

Lars Kolind

throughout Denmark.) The so-called spaghetti structure reduces hierarchy, opens up multiple channels of simultaneous communication among workers, and exposes employees to some of the responsibilities that other workers deal with.

Developing and implementing the spaghetti organization was a creative act on the human resource level. But even before Kolind arrived at this managerial solution, he had improved his company's most important product, hearing aids, through another act of moral imagination. His sources of inspiration have much in common with those that the other business leaders in this book have drawn upon for their innovations.

When Kolind became the CEO of Oticon Corporation, after many years in operational roles such as production planning, logistics, operations research, and middle management, he took a fresh look at the company's chief line of products. Oticon long had a reputation for producing the most powerful and scientifically advanced hearing aids on the market. The company's high-quality hearing aids had been called nothing short of "wondrous" by experts on sound waves and the ear's auditory capacities. But Kolind was less interested in technical quality than in the client's needs. He told me that he was thinking along these lines at the time: "The ear itself is not our client; it is not our customer. Our client is the whole person. And our goal is to make our clients smile. That's what we want to do."

Kolind emphasized that from early in life his "values were all about respecting [people] for what they were," a perspective closely aligned with his moral beliefs. Kolind's passion outside the realm of work is scouting, which in Denmark, he says, is "pretty much associated with the church, and church is part of being a scout." The moral commitments that Kolind acquired while engaged in service to church and scouting shaped his moral imagination, which in turn gave Kolind the creative insights that he needed to reform both the products and the organizational structure of his company.

Kolind's love and respect for people "as they are" led him to question whether the powerful hearing aids that Oticon was selling best served the human needs of hearing-impaired people. "We actually went out for the first time and asked real people," he recalled. "Just ordinary questions of quality of life. What is it that disturbs your quality of life? What is it that you really want?" Kolind's intuitive insights into the real needs of the hearing impaired had given him a sense that they were not comfortable with even the best of Oticon's products, and these intuitions were confirmed: "No one ever asked for the world's most advanced hearing aid. People asked for quality of life."

Quality of life for the hearing impaired called for a device that could be worn with minimal attention, not one that gave maximum sound to the ear: it is the whole person that counts in the end, not some technical measure of auditory performance. Although the technical excellence of Oticon hearing aids remained essential, this standard was now accompanied by another priority, one that came directly from the consumers' own wishes: "They did not want maximum speech intelligibility in noise. They wanted a combination of good speech intelligibility, small instrument, and comfortable sound. Until then, the method had been to measure the sound that actually hits the tympanic membrane. And if that matches a theoretical curve, then the hearing aid is perfect. And if it does not, it's not perfect. I figured out that the only disadvantage of that method, which is quite scientifically wonderful, is that it works equally good whether the patient is dead or alive. And I said, 'I'm not sure that's the right criterion for quality. So now let's develop something that works on live persons.'"

Naturally Kolind's new approach met stiff resistance among some technicians, engineers, and board members at Oticon, but he persevered and won the argument in the end. The results for the company were nothing less than spectacular: Oticon's smaller, sleeker hearing aids with the more "comfortable" sound became the industry standard overnight. The Oticon hearing aids won overwhelming market share by combining the technical excellence that they were known for with a new consumer appeal. Kolind was on his way to becoming a legend in the European business community.

What sealed Kolind's renown was the "spaghetti" organization that he designed to transform employee relations at Oticon and other companies that he later directed. During his struggle to make Oticon more attuned to its customers' "whole-person" needs, Kolind realized that he needed to think about the structural reasons that his company was overlooking such crucial concerns, and why it was resistant to constructive feedback and change. "I realized that Oticon would have functioned not because of its structure but despite its structure," he said. "And we would have functioned better with no form of structure whatsoever, because there was a very, very efficient informal structure. And why not make that one the formal structure? So that was the spaghetti organization, basically—it was a structure in which there was lots of freedom."

Some of the features of the spaghetti organization were installed as a direct response to problems that Kolind had run into while fighting for his "revolutionary" (his word) hearing aid concept. For example, he introduced a management strategy of requiring employees to serve in multiple roles (engineers as marketers, accountants in customer service, and so on) as a way of sensitizing everyone in the company to the entire complexity of a client's needs. "I had a lot of conflict with everybody," he noted, "so I said, 'Let's turn more jobs into multi-jobs.' And [with] multi-jobs . . . you have a portfolio of functions . . . because we want you to understand the whole business and not only your aspect of the business."

Other features came from Kolind's knowledge of people. He tore down the company hierarchy to liberate the most talented people, allowing them to do their best work as well as inspire others. "I know we lose some coordination, we lose some focus by abandoning the hierarchy," he said. "But we will gain 50 percent, and all our most valuable people can now start to do something productive. And that was why I abandoned [a formal hierarchy] and substituted for it a very un-hierarchical structure . . . where everybody had a mentor and they chose themselves who should be their mentor . . . and these 'gurus' would have a right to command, but they would create an atmosphere around them, a professional atmosphere that should inspire everybody to do better from a professional point of view."

Giving people this kind of freedom requires some basic assumptions about human potential, a vision reflecting optimism and trust. In flattening and extending the company's organization, Kolind treated employees more like peers than underlings, spreading responsibilities throughout the company in unprecedented ways. This is not done lightly by any CEO. That Kolind was able to stick with his creative vision indicates how deep-seated his sense of trust was in fellow employees. It also indicates the extent to which his passion for Denmark's church-linked scouting movement influenced his thinking. The moral imagination that enabled Kolind to invent and implement his spaghetti model sprang directly from his faith in the scouting way of operating. "I, frankly speaking, got 90 percent of the inspiration [for the spaghetti organization] from scouting. . . . Scouting has been my whole life," he said. "And what struck me was that we could do anything with minimal resources or no resources fundamentally. Because we agreed on the fundamentals, and there were some very simple fundamental rules . . . the Scout Law, the Scout Promise. So we had a common ground, and we were committed to get things done."

Kolind appropriated the scouting approach to the high reaches of corporation management because he was convinced that the fundamentals of human relations were the same: if people can be given freedom and trust, they will work to their fullest potential—provided, of course, that they are committed and talented people. Kolind carefully selected and retained such people and then built his organization in a free-flowing manner that unleashed their best work. His own moral commitments gave him the insight to do this and the temerity to see it through in the face of severe skepticism. "So, while many people within the company and outside the company said, 'This will never work,' I, frankly speaking, never doubted it would work. This doesn't mean I wasn't afraid we wouldn't fail from a commercial point of view, because we didn't have enough money or whatever it was. But it was fundamentally right. And you might say, 'Why was that?' I think it was like that because decisions of that sort, fundamental decisions, have been made more by the heart than by the brain."

When the heart and brain are in alignment, powerful forces are unleashed, forces of creativity, purpose, persistence in the face of skepticism, strong ethical commitments, compassion, and leadership. I will discuss these forces in detail throughout this book. One revered business leader who not only has exemplified these forces in his own career but also has written about some of them (in particular, leadership) is Max DePree, whom I interviewed at his lakeside home in northern Michigan.

In addition to being one of the most revered businesspeople of our time, Max DePree is a best-selling, insightful writer on moral leadership in business. Among his many other honors, DePree has been elected to *Fortune* magazine's Business Hall of Fame. In 1980 he became the chief executive officer of the Herman Miller office furniture company, and on his watch the company was ranked seventh out of the *Fortune* 500 in profitability (return to investors) and first in productivity (net income generated per employee). How did DePree squeeze so much productiveness out of his workforce? Not exactly through blood, sweat, and tears. Early in his tenure as the CEO, DePree convinced the company to introduce an employee stock-ownership plan, sharing a part of its capital wealth with its workers. At the time, this was a revolutionary notion and would not have been an easy sell in many corporate boardrooms. It took the business world some time to recognize that directly including all workers in a company's financial prospects can be an enlightened way of promoting company interests, with propitious effects on morale, loyalty, and ultimately (as in Herman Miller's case) productivity.

When I spoke with DePree about his career, he identified the stock-sharing plan that he created at Herman Miller as his proudest

Max DePree

achievement. Of his four-decades-long career as a top executive, legendary CEO, and best-selling author, it was this early initiative during his chairmanship that DePree recalled as his finest hour:

> Oh, one of the things that I'm most proud of is that almost everybody at Herman Miller is a stockholder. That's one thing that gives me real, real pleasure today. I ran into a guy at a drugstore a few months ago. I hadn't seen him in maybe ten years. He works in the factory at Herman Miller, and I said, "I'm glad to see you."
>
> He said, "I've been planning to give you a call." And I said, "Well fine, what about?" He said, "Can we talk here?" We were both waiting for a prescription to be filled, and I said, "Yeah, sure." He said, "I wanted to tell you, years ago when you started that program of stock ownership for all of us . . . I thought, 'Oh that's *another* one of Max's "ideas."' We sat around the coffee table and we laughed about it." [The man] said, "I want you to know today, I'm really well-off and I'm going to have a retirement I never dreamed I could have, because you made me a stockholder."
>
> But you see, I never gave him anything; he earned it all. I mean, the stock they get, they can buy at a discount, but the quarterly profit-sharing is paid in stock, since we're a public company. So nobody gave him anything. He just got the opportunity to earn it.

DePree's modest perspective on his own contribution to his workers' well-being ("I never gave him anything; he earned it all") indicates the sense of humility that, perhaps paradoxically, characterizes many top business leaders. One of the essentials of good leadership is keeping perspective on the power that your position grants you. The best way to do this is to remember that the power is in the position, not in your own intrinsic superiority to others; and that it is a power meant to serve others, not to dominate them.

We shall return to this view later in the chapter, when I discuss the case of Robert Greenleaf, the founder of an enlightened model of business management called "servant leadership." DePree has long been a fan of Greenleaf's writings and the servant-leadership model. In DePree's own book *Leadership Is an Art* he urges readers to think about leadership as "stewardship as contrasted with ownership."[1] He cites two sources of personal inspiration: the Gospel of Luke, where the leader is described as "one who serves," and Greenleaf's work *Servant Leadership,* commenting that Greenleaf "has written an excellent book about this idea."[2] Greenleaf, in his own modest manner, always credited previous sources with the idea, even though it was his own writings that first introduced people in business to the servant-leader approach.

True to the ethic of humility, DePree acknowledges debts to his intellectual mentors for initiatives such as the employee stock-ownership plan. DePree sees such ideas as growing naturally out of his deep respect for all the company's employees, a view that embodies the servant-leader model. While this may be a moral imperative in biblical and other religious traditions, in DePree's hands the notion carried great practical value as well.

In this concept, the leader learns from subordinates just as they learn from him or her. Indeed, a company's prosperity depends on its staff's capacity to learn in *both* directions, from supervisor to subordinate and vice versa. When DePree reflects on this two-way process, his account is imbued with a double dose of humility: he attributes his realization that his subordinates often knew more than he did to a mentor, the industrial psychologist Carl Frost; and the realization itself centers on the benefits of a humble stance toward those who report to a leader. "I don't think I would have figured it out," he said, "You know, maybe Einstein figured out the theory of relativity by sitting on his duff and musing on it, but I think most of us learn by interaction. We teach each other a lot and if we're open to it, we really learn a lot. One of the crucial things in my management training was when Carl Frost . . . told me when I was a young manager one time, 'When you have problems running a factory and you don't know what to do, you go out in the factory and you ask the people who are working in the factory.' He said, 'They always know what to do, but nobody ever asks them.' And I thought, well, the least I can do is try that, and it works!"

In *Some Do Care*, the book that Anne Colby and I wrote about living American moral exemplars, we found exactly this kind of learning from followers among the leaders whom we studied.[3] At the time, this amazed us, because we had assumed that it was leaders who defined moral causes and initiated social action. But instead we found moral leadership to be a back-and-forth, two-way street, much like the kind of "interaction" that DePree describes in the servant-as-leader approach to business management.

We noted that one of the characteristics of inspirational moral leaders was their "capacity to take direction, as well as social support, from their followers."[4] For example, Andrei Sakharov, the Nobel Prize-winning human rights spokesperson, commented that his followers sometimes had to bring him "kicking and screaming" to a new cause that he had been slow to recognize. Once he adopted the cause, however, his own leadership skills galvanized the group and were key in carrying the day for the cause. But he would not have discovered the issue unless he had been willing and able to take direction from those who normally took direction from him. This temporary role reversal, the capacity to listen and learn as well as to inspire, is the paradox of the servant-leader.

The employee stock-ownership program that DePree instituted at Herman Miller was of great practical value to the company. As noted, however, DePree did not see this share-the-wealth plan simply as a moral imperative. If the plan had not been in the enlightened self-interests of those who controlled the company, DePree could never have persuaded the board to go along with it—and indeed it would have made poor business sense. But DePree was not oblivious to the salutary moral implications of the plan. He under-

stood that good acts and good business go hand in hand. A successful business leader uses good acts to promote the company's interests, rather than needing to trade them off against one another. In
another paradox, *both* moral goals and business goals are primary
and inviolable: the leader is always committed to the promotion
and integration of moral and business goals. This is what I referred
to in the book's introduction as the necessarily mixed motives of
those who are able to succeed in business over the long haul.

In yet another extension of Herman Miller's innovative
employee stock-ownership program, DePree developed what he
called a "silver parachute" to discourage hostile takeover attempts.
As with the stock-ownership program, this had a highly practical
intention, namely to keep control of the company in the hands of its
current board. But at the same time, DePree was compelled by the
plan's moral basis in fairness. Unlike other executives at the time, he
did not support a "golden parachute" plan that rewarded only a few
of the top bosses. DePree's "silver" solution better addressed both the
moral and the business goals that he was committed to. In his explanation of the program below, note the way that DePree fully integrates the two types of motives:

> Then another thing we did that's a variation on that theme,
> you know Herman Miller at [that] time was exposed to hostile
> takeovers, in the late seventies, early eighties, like a lot of compa-
> nies were. There's a lot in the literature about golden parachutes.
> So we invented a silver parachute. What we did is we said you
> can't defend the equity of having five or six people at the top who
> get a golden parachute in the case of a hostile takeover; you can
> only defend it if a whole category of people in the company get
> some kind of a parachute. So we said, once you've been at
> Herman Miller for a year, you join the silver parachute group. If
> there's a hostile takeover, you'll be compensated in relation to how
> long you've been with the company and how much you were
> paid.
>
> Now, this did two things actually. I mean, it was the fair thing
> to do in terms of all those people. It also put an extra cost on the
> back of the acquirer. If they really wanted to take you over, they
> had to pay that cost, which helped to inhibit the idea that you

could take us over. But you see, it wasn't primarily designed to prevent a takeover. It was primarily designed to bring equity.

When a person is able to integrate moral and business goals in so thorough a manner, it is a hallmark of what is commonly called *integrity.* (After all, the root term in *integration* and *integrity* are the same.) No one acquires personal integrity overnight. It is achieved in small steps, over years of character development. Integrity develops as part of an entire awareness of what matters in life—a setting of priorities that positions purpose and meaning in their rightful places, as the overall goals that should drive everything else. DePree speaks for many of the subjects detailed in this book when he describes how this awareness gradually dawned on him during his career:

> I had a lot of the normal focus and let's say "driving attributes" that most younger people have when they set out in a business career. I can remember a time, standing in front of all the management team at Herman Miller, and talking about how important it was to have a good quarter. And, of course, nobody gives a hoot today how good the quarters were when I was CEO, nobody ever asks me, "What kind of quarters did you have?"—and I don't worry about it either! But I think that, for me, one of the very important things that happened in the course of a business career was the slow discovery that business and businesspeople have to be a positive part of society, and that I had to be very serious about the human side of all that was happening in the business world.
>
> You see, that comes back to the question in life, not just business, but in life, which is "What will you measure?" And money is fairly easy to measure. . . . But leadership is a function of questions. And the first question for a leader always is: "Who do we intend to be?" Not "What are we going to do?" but "Who do we intend to be?"

DePree's "Who do we intend to be?" is one example of the "why" questions that I began this book with: Why pursue this objective? Why behave in this manner? Why aspire to this kind of life? Why become this kind of person? As DePree rightly says, these are broad questions that are not as easy to answer as might be a quantitative question such as "What can we measure?" For this reason, they are often dismissed or relegated to marginalized, compartmentalized occasions in life, such as meditation or worship. But for DePree and the other leaders highlighted in this book, the big questions permeate everything, including all the day-to-day decisions about how to manage a business.

It is not that quantitative measures are overlooked—business, after all, is about making money, and none of the leaders in this book would have succeeded without keeping close track of that—but rather that the significance of the quantitative measures is understood in light of the big questions, *rather than the other way around*. This is not merely an academic distinction. It changes the entire way in which the company makes decisions. Keeping the big questions in mind enables a company to resist the inevitable pressures toward short-term results in favor of a more beneficial long-term perspective. When temptations to act unethically arise, the "why" questions help people keep their bearings, placing the ill-gotten gain in the context of their real goals and interests. Sometimes this is the only way that businesspeople can find the strength to resist an easy but shady profit; and it can literally save the day, preventing eventual damage that would far overwhelm any gain that had been made.

At the company level, the best work a leader can do is to communicate the importance of the big "why" questions throughout the ranks. This is what it means to make sure that employees not only understand the company's mission but also that they know how to act in a way that promotes that mission. When such understanding is widely distributed in a company, leadership itself becomes shared, because workers can be counted on to make good decisions without constant supervision.

DePree, in his conversation with me, noted an example of this. He commented on how simple a matter it was for one of his employees to turn down a commonplace unethical proposition that has snagged huge numbers of companies in painful scandals. Resisting this alluring trap was easy because of the clear standards that DePree set for Herman Miller behavior: "One of our senior salespeople was dealing with an important decision-maker at [un-named company]. We were talking about it, and my recollection is that it was about a $12 million order. And the guy said, 'Well, I can arrange for you to have this order, but we have to talk about what my share is going to be.' And our man said, 'Well, there isn't going to be any share for you. Our company doesn't do this.' 'Sure,' the guy said, 'everybody does it.' 'No,' [our man] said, 'we don't.' And [their man] said, 'Well, I'm going to have to call your boss, and you'll probably lose your job.' And [our man] said, 'Oh no, we just lose the order.' Because he knew that's what I would say."

This story had a happy financial ending: the unnamed company made the deal anyway. Yet DePree would have accepted his employee's actions even if they had not been accompanied by an immediate monetary victory: "And we got the order, because the guy couldn't go back to his superior and explain why he wasn't able to give the low bidder the order. But in a case like that, [our man] had to know me quite well in order to just put that on the line, and say, 'Well, we can lose the order. We can live with that.' I think one of the jobs of leaders is to make that very clear to people in the organization."

"Making things clear to people in the organization" is an ele-mentary skill expected of any executive, DePree suggests. In business-school language this is known generally as "communication skills." While it is certainly that, there is something about the "skills" lan-guage that fails to capture what it really takes to convince one's busi-ness colleagues—even if they are subordinates—to share one's vision of a company's best path forward. No one stays inspired for long merely on the basis of a skillful presentation. The message must have a center that holds, a moral center that addresses the com-pany's responsibilities to the entire community of stakeholders, a center that has an interest in how the company operates. More than rhetorical skills, communicating such a message requires a deep understanding of how the company serves its customers, what the company offers to its investors, how the company should treat its employees, what kind of corporate citizen the company should be, and what the company contributes to society at large.

Such a comprehensive moral sense permeates essentially every communiqué issued by a great business leader. This is no accident or public relations trick. Rather, the moral sense is the source of the ideas that move one's colleagues to pull in the right direction, and in this sense it is the heart and soul of one's leadership.

In his interview for this book, DePree shows how the direction that he set for Herman Miller, and then powerfully communicated throughout the company ranks, reflected his sense of what best served *everyone* affected by the company's work. Consistent with the fundamental theme of this book, DePree refused to accept trade-offs between the interests of different stakeholders—or, to put it in a broader sense, between the company's quest for profits and its responsibility to treat all the people it dealt with fairly:

> You've got your customers, and you've got your shareholders, and you've got all the people who work in the corporation, and you've got your communities. You're always a part of a community. I don't think that I ever had the feeling that in order to solve the needs of one group, you hurt the needs of another. I never felt that that's where it ended up. I always felt that a lot of that is fairly rational and, you know, when we talked about establishing a pension plan for instance, we didn't see it as taking away something from the shareholders, or as being a cost we couldn't collect from a customer.
>
> We made some decisions about costs in the company on the basis of whether it was in some cases ethical to charge a customer for it. But I don't remember those as being a difficult problem. In the contest between how much an employee gets out of the company and how much a shareholder gets out of the company, you know there are pretty rational ways to think about that, because after all you're all pretty much in the same boat. Everybody needs to have a certain level of performance in order to be able to continue as a part of the team.

Not only must the leader's directives be morally centered in the sense that they consider the company's responsibilities to all those whose lives are touched by the company but also they must conform to the moral imperative of honesty. Truthfulness is the greatest divider of businesspeople who accomplish something real in their careers and those whose work adds up to nothing more than pretense, fakery, or just getting by. It is the most demanding standard in good business, because the pressures to misrepresent results are never-ending. But in the long run, honesty is also the most rewarding standard, providing the incomparable moral advantage of trustworthiness.

Benjamin Franklin was right: "Honesty is the best policy." Although he was expressing an unequivocal moral standard, he was being neither moralistic nor idealistic. Franklin's explicit point in *Poor Richard's Almanac* was that honesty has a proven *practical* value. He was offering his young readers the best way to get ahead, not a sermon.

Another iconoclastic American who was just as clear about the practical value of honesty was P. T. Barnum. Although he gained notoriety for his avid pursuit of fame and wealth, in fact he introduced a number of clean business practices to the tawdry circuses of his day. In a Barnum circus, unlike virtually all the others, the games of chance were run fairly, pickpockets were arrested rather than sanctioned by the management (who were typically on the take), and customers were given correct change when they made purchases. The success of the Barnum circuses flowed directly from what became known as their "Sunday school" reputation. Barnum's explanation: "As a matter of mere selfishness, honesty is the best policy." His advice to aspiring businesspeople was far from the cynical maxims falsely attributed to him (for example, "There's a sucker born every minute"). Instead, Barnum warned, "It is the most difficult thing in life to make money dishonestly . . . [because] no man can be dishonest without soon being found out. When his lack of principles is discovered, nearly every avenue to success is closed against him forever."[5]

In a similar vein, DePree explains the importance of honesty in all of one's communications. He notes that trust is the essential aim of which a businessperson must never lose sight. But DePree's experience made him realistic: honesty is easier said than done in the business world. That is why it is crucial to always keep in mind the practical value of truth-telling, as well as the real and irreversible penalties, to one's career and one's sense of self that inevitably follow deceit. This is a theme that I shall return to many times in this book, as leaders and followers alike grapple with the pivotal challenge of maintaining honesty and integrity in the face of severe pressures to distort, conceal, exaggerate, and even lie or cheat. DePree describes how he repeated this theme over and over to the workers who reported to him when he was Herman Miller's CEO:

> Another thing that I deal with is people who say to me, "I've been trying to communicate the best I can but people don't seem to understand." And I say, "Well, are you telling them the truth?" They say, "Well, you know, you can't always tell them everything." I say, "That isn't what my question is. My question is 'Are you telling them the truth?'" Well, then they start to deal with that problem and they often confess, "Well, I haven't told them the whole truth." And then I say, "Well, why not?" I mean, these are people you trust and they trust you. Why aren't you telling them the whole truth? How can the truth hurt you? And if the truth can hurt you, then you have another problem." So that's the kind of thing that comes up often. People say, "Gee, it's a communications problem." I say, "No, it's a truth problem."

DePree, like most who make it to the top of the business world and manage to stay there for more than a few shaky moments, understands clearly the inextricable coupling between truthfulness and trust. He knows what too many fallen leaders have forgotten—or perhaps never truly realized: "Well, you can't run a good organization without trust, and you can't have trust without truth. People are not dummies. They always know what's going on."

In the business management literature, there have been reams written about strategies for effective communication as a prime leadership tool. But effective communication is far more than a strategy: it is a way of imparting genuine insight and inspiration to people with whom one shares a relationship of mutual respect. It is a moral act, driven by the intent of all parties to traffic in the truth and thereby define and strive for a goal that benefits all. Communication for a great leader like DePree derives directly from such moral concerns, including his respect for the people with whom he is communicating. It is his way of getting them on board a ship that will take them to where they all want to go. It is *not* a means of manipulating them to act in ways that serve one's narrow, immediate interests—a self-defeating trap to which "strategic thinking" without a moral center can lead. Communication is a means of building human relationships that are valued in themselves, not a way of using people merely as a means toward some other end.

DePree credits two of his intellectual mentors with this insight that guided his personnel practices as a corporate executive: "I think the thing that I learned primarily from Carl Frost and David Hubbard, over the years, was that in organized activity, you can be technically competent, and that's a wonderful advantage, but you can't realize your potential until you know how to establish and nurture relationships. I think that the problems in organized activity have much more to do with the relationship side of life than with the technical-competent side of life. I think that leadership really requires the ability to develop really good relationships, because then you can manage the trade-offs and the disagreements."

The capacity for such leadership certainly draws on managerial skill and what DePree calls "the technical-competent side of life." But that is only part of the story, and an insufficient part at that. At its core, the capacity comes from the firm and abiding moral sense that since the days of the early Greek philosophers has been named *character*. Quite literally, the Greek root of the word means "imprinted" or "stamped upon." A person with moral character acts as if virtues such as honesty and compassion had been stamped into his or her personality—that's why we feel that we can rely on that person to do the right thing, day in and day out. Integrity, or "wholeness" in its root form, is a direct function of moral character. People who are always in touch with their moral sentiments, and who are committed to acting in accord with these sentiments, behave with an almost tangible coherence in their daily lives. Their character and integrity drink from the same moral spring.

When considering sources of personal inspiration, it is impossible to speak of morality without bringing up the matter of religious faith. Many people—not all, but many—find their moral guidance from a religious doctrine, either learned as children from their parents or discovered in midlife. In some populations, morality and religious faith almost always go hand in hand. For example, when Anne Colby and I studied living American moral exemplars who had dedicated their entire lives to good works, we found that more than 80 percent of these people credited their extraordinary moral commitments to their religious convictions.[6] In a study of American journalists who display a strong moral sense (yes, highly moral journalists do still exist, and in significant numbers), however, we found relatively few who said that their religious beliefs have influenced their work.[7]

People in business may be on the higher end of the spectrum in their linking of morality with religion. Many men and women profiled in this book, for example—not all, but many—describe themselves as people of strong religious faith. Often this is not something that is widely known about them, especially around their offices, because these leaders resist using their positions in ways that might seem discriminatory or otherwise inappropriate to their subordinates. But they speak about their faith with close friends and peers from the ranks of the business leadership community. My conversation with DePree shed light on this phenomenon, both in the way he attributes his character to his faith and to the way he has used it—quietly—on the job to shore up his moral commitments. As illustrated in the interview excerpt below, DePree's experience in the business world at large suggests that many other business leaders share his orientation, if not his particular doctrinal faith:

DePree: Church was a very important part of our social life growing up. Sure, that has a lot to do with the character side of it. These beliefs strongly influence the practices later on in life. . . . I pray about decisions, I pray about problems, and I pray about the problems that other people have, more for other people than for me. Over my working life, I would pray about things.

Interviewer: You did mention right at the beginning [of the interview] too about the relationship between work and faith.

DePree: Yes.

Interviewer: You know, it is interesting because it comes up a lot from a variety of different faiths in business leaders, whether it's Judaism or Christianity or whatever.

DePree: Sure, yes, one of my experiences that I have always found kind of interesting is that when you are at conferences and continuing education programs of senior leaders and CEOs, when you get together over a cocktail or dinner in the evening, there's a lot of talk about that.

Interviewer: Is that right?

DePree: Yeah, there's a lot of congruence, whether you're Jewish or Catholic or Protestant or whatever. The discussions about beliefs and faith are—you know, with the inside guys, there's a lot of it. That's been *my* experience.

As mentioned earlier in this chapter, Robert Greenleaf was the pioneering spirit behind a revolutionary management approach known as "servant leadership." Simply put, Greenleaf's idea was that leaders—including the most powerful corporate bosses—should think of themselves as servants first and foremost. Their leadership must be conducted in the spirit oriented toward service if it is to be beneficial and effective in the long run. Greenleaf did not mean this only as a moral statement, although he was concerned with ethics. More pointedly, he made it as a claim about what makes a successful and enduring leader.

Greenleaf's radical notion was that adopting an attitude of service can help leaders gain the capacity to accomplish what they want, both for themselves and for the groups that they lead. There should be no trade-offs between service and success, between authority and democracy, between power and humility—in Greenleaf's imagination, all these horses pull together. His visionary writings have influenced many cutting-edge management theorists, from Peter Senge to Max DePree, and they have spawned a Center for Servant-Leadership in his name. This is all the more remarkable given Greenleaf's late start as a writer. He began putting his thoughts to paper only after a long management career at AT&T. Greenleaf retired at age sixty and began the most productive phase of his theorizing after a five-year period of study and reflection. Although the revolution in leadership attitude that Greenleaf imagined is still a long way from becoming a universal reality, it has made

Robert Greenleaf

solid inroads among the managerial ranks of many important corporations.

I interviewed Robert Greenleaf, when he was eighty-four, two years before his death. To see him, I traveled the back roads of rural Pennsylvania to an assisted-living community where Greenleaf was well cared for but mentally restless. Active of mind and still eager to contribute his wisdom to the public good, he was unhappy with the way our society puts its elderly on a shelf to dry up and wither away. Nor was he pleased with the direction that corporate America was taking. At that time, there had been some highly publicized scandals, and everyone was trying to revive business ethics; indeed, Greenleaf's own writings on ethical behavior in business were receiving increased attention. But whatever impact he may have had, Greenleaf told me, there was still much to be done. "I guess part of the problem I have in the modern resurgence concerning this business of ethics," he said, "is that we don't really know how to deal with it any better than we did twenty-five years ago."

I learned two insights from Greenleaf that have stayed with me since that interview. The first is that real success can be achieved only by aiming to accomplish a big and elevated purpose—one that goes beyond self-advancement and material gratification. Greenleaf aimed for success in every possible sense: sense of accomplishment, sense of self-fulfillment, sense of satisfaction, sense of moral contribution, and sense of personal pleasure that one gets from a job well done. Personal and material successes are parts of it, but these always must be kept in perspective; and they are truly satisfying only when they come along with all the other accomplishments. Greenleaf did not even distinguish between moral and personal goals: he believed that good work in business brings both kinds of rewards.

The second great insight is that the path to this kind of all-around success begins with an act of discovery. We need to get in touch with *all* our motives, from the mundane to the spiritual, to know how to pursue them *all* without giving up—or, as Greenleaf might say, "losing focus" during those inevitable high-pressure times when things seem so complicated that we become tempted to let go of our most noble aspirations. Greenleaf's focus, that which he urged people to never lose, was on a *why* question and a *what* question, considered simultaneously: *Why* are you doing this? *What* do you really want to accomplish, or *what* is your true purpose here? In the fast-paced flux of today's business world, this essential focus is often lost, or perhaps never even achieved.

Greenleaf told me, more with a tone of regret than criticism: "There are an awful lot of people around wondering why they're here. And I just wonder how they got into that state, but they did. And I sometimes feel that they get a little lost, a little unfocused. They forget why they are doing what they're doing, or they give up on it. They may decide that it's more realistic to just get by. I don't really think much that way [myself] . . . but I'm aware that there's a lot of these people around who need this kind of focus." Greenleaf started with questions of purpose—Why are you in business? What do you want to achieve?—and assumed that sensible answers to such questions must include a sense of service. Business is always about serving someone, and in the end the success of any business is measured by the value of that service.

Greenleaf was by no means alone in pointing out the importance of purpose and service for aspiring business leaders. The value of aiming high and pursuing big, noble, larger-than-life goals was trumpeted loud and clear by James Collins and Jerry Porras's *Built to Last,* the classic comparison between growing and declining businesses. Collins and Porras identified the "BHAG" (a "big, hairy, audacious goal") as the most essential ingredient for achieving enduring success.[8] And capitalists back to Adam Smith often have noted that an ethic of service lies at the heart of any good business.[9]

But what Greenleaf in particular showed us was the *personal* consequences that accrue when businesspeople pursue noble purposes and adopt the ethic of service. Such choices may require a transformation in how you understand the priorities of your career, a view more toward the far horizon than the immediate bumps in the road. Happily, the transformation does not require sacrificing any of your work ambitions: to the contrary, it creates a win-win condition that enables people to meet all their career goals. But it does require steady commitment, strong values, and a genuine belief in the importance of what you are doing—something akin to an act of faith, repeated each time you go to work.

By the time I interviewed Greenleaf, he already had become a guru for business leaders inspired by his vision of the servant-leader, and his reputation was still growing rapidly. Yet Greenleaf went out of his way to tell me that he had not originated the concept for which he had become famous. Rather, he said that he got the idea for servant leadership from Herman Hesse's *Journey to the East*, and he pointed out that the same idea could be found in many sources of traditional wisdom, including the Bible. As for his own contribution, Greenleaf said, "I don't feel that I've done that much with it except sort of give a new twist to servant as leader."

Of course Greenleaf's "new twist" was responsible for the concept's applicability to modern business management; and without his reworking of the idea, few in business today would have any inkling that leadership is best understood as a form of service. But Greenleaf was not showing false modesty when he made that comment. It was real humility, not some disingenuous act. He did take credit for one virtue that made all the difference in getting the business world to take notice of the vision that he held dear: "I just don't get discouraged easily." True humility does not imply shyness or self-deprecation; rather, it goes hand in hand with confidence and purpose.

Service, humility, ethics, faith—these are hardly the qualities that the public has come to associate with successful business leaders. Yet they have been recognized and recommended by observers of business before, especially by those who have experienced business from the inside. Why these recommendations have been so often ignored or resisted is a matter that I shall take up in subsequent chapters.

In this chapter, I have identified some of the personal characteristics that endow a business career with a "moral advantage." I have discussed these characteristics in the context of three "leading lights" of the business world: Lars Kolind, Max DePree, and Robert Greenleaf. The three are different from one another in a host of ways, including their particular talents and interests, and they each took their own path to self-discovery and building moral character. But they shared the sense that this was their ultimate aim, and that business success would come as a result of their loftier aspirations rather than in disregard or in spite of them. Each leader shared commitments to humility, trust, leadership as a service, truth in communication, and to authority based on respect for those whom one leads. Each man shared a dedication to ethics, integrity, and in the cases of Kolind and DePree, to their faith.

These leaders also shared a devotion to the entire community within and surrounding their businesses—the investors, partners, clients, customers, employees, neighbors, and the broader society that their work has served. In this regard, Kolind, DePree, and Greenleaf personify the age-old notion of "work as a calling," the unique service to the world that every person is given the privilege to perform. When people are able to think about their work in this way, they are already on their way to finding their work meaningful and rewarding. The sense that work in business has significance beyond survival and gain provides an advantage that endures through all the ups and downs of a career. In the forthcoming chapters, we shall now explore the many faces of that "moral advantage."

2 The Moral Advantage

> I tell you that virtue is not given by money,
> but that from virtue comes money, and
> every other good, public as well as private.

SOCRATES

When I titled this book *The Moral Advantage,* I was aware that the phrase could sound both naive and crass, not an appealing combination. On the naive-sounding side, am I really claiming that morality in business is a way of advancing one's *own* interests, of actually creating an *advantage* for oneself? If I am making such a claim in earnest, this idea surely seems a bit clueless in a world where CEOs make off with vast fortunes by inflating their pay, hanging employees out to dry, and deceiving the public: clearly you don't need to be moral to make a lot of money. On the crass-sounding side, am I promoting the idea that morality should be viewed merely as a means to advance our own interests?

My answer to the first question is yes, I *am* claiming that morality is the best pathway to business success, the surest means of promoting both one's own career interests and the interests of those with whom one does business. But I am referring to a kind of success that is broader and more satisfying than monetary gain alone—although financial success is certainly included in the vision that I have in mind.

My answer to the second question is no, I am *not* claiming that morality's main purpose is to promote one's narrow self-interests. Moral conduct is an end in itself, not reducible to any reward that it might or might not bring. In business, if there is a choice between doing the right thing and making a profit, the moral choice must be to do the right thing. And such choices do arise in business, as in any other area of life. Yet even in such cases, the moral choice has a way of yielding benefits in the end. Some of these benefits are personal: the sense of satisfaction that one gets from pride in good work, the sense of integrity that one gets from a commitment to high standards and noble purposes. Such personal benefits are rewarding in themselves, and they also contribute to long-term career success by bolstering one's inspiration and motivation. People who believe in their work feel good about it, and when they feel this way, they are likely to acquire greater energy, talent, imagination, and staying power.

In this chapter, I show the many distinct ways that morality can contribute to business success. Some of these ways are familiar (following ethical codes, for example), whereas others (such as unleashing the powers of moral imagination) have seldom been described, at least in a systematic manner. My aim here is to develop a framework of business morality that will give readers a new understanding of how morality actually works in building a rewarding career.

The Cynical View of Morality in Business

As a prelude to presenting the framework, I must acknowledge that many people these days are likely to be skeptical of my claims about the relationship between morality and success. Cynicism about what it takes to get ahead in business has become prevalent both within and outside the business world, so much so that I have taken as one of the secondary goals of this book the hopes of combating this cynicism: after all, a pervasive belief in the inevitability of moral degeneracy can become self-fulfilling.

Here's the cynical line that I hope to challenge: *"Sure, every now and then a corrupt businessperson gets in trouble by being caught with his or her hands in the till, and in that sense it's true that blatant immorality can destroy success. But the most advantageous course of action is to find a way to get away with it, to do whatever it takes to make the most money without getting caught. As for morality itself— those limits and rules, that nagging voice of conscience, the stifling demands of prudence and reputation—for anyone in business with a sharp eye on the bottom line, it feels more like a ball and chain than some sort of advantage."*

Ask any group of sophisticated people who take pride in their hard-nosed hold on reality (journalists would be one such group, lawyers another), and you will find a good sampling of the following opinions:

1. Moneymaking generally is tainted by avarice, deceit, or exploitation.

2. A show of ethics may be required from time to time, because it helps to have customers and employees think that they are being treated fairly. But cheating works fine when people aren't looking.

3. Ethical conduct is like an unpleasant medicine that society forces down businesspeople's throats to protect the world from their avarice.

4. Morality just gets in the way of the cold, hard actions that truly ambitious people must take to reach their goals.

5. The quest for profits necessarily stands in conflict with efforts to be fair, decent, and charitable.

6. In business, the only sensible time for salving the conscience and soothing the moral sense is "at the end of the day," at the close of a successful career, when you can give back some of those ill-gotten gains with some high-profile philanthropy.

Such skepticism about moneymaking goes back a long way, filling the annals of religious and literary writing. The Bible, of course, warned that it may be harder for a rich man to enter the kingdom of heaven than for a camel to pass through a needle's eye, referring to the corruption of character that can result from the zeal of acquisitiveness. Along these lines, British author G. K. Chesterton once noted that "a businessman is the only man who is forever apologizing for his occupation." And Balzac, famously, wrote: "Behind every great fortune lies a great crime."[1]

From the less lofty perch of mass culture, the view is much the same. More often than not, popular media characterize business as nothing more than a self-serving exercise in greed, carried out in as corrupt and ruthless a manner as the businessperson can get away with. In television and movies, moneymaking in business is almost always seen as a greedy affair. One study of how television treats business leaders found that "a majority of the CEOs portrayed on prime time have committed felonies."[2] Another study found that by a ratio of more than two to one, Hollywood portrays business leaders in a negative rather than a positive light. The unflattering portrayals have become even more pointed over time: *Wall Street*'s irredeemable Gordon Gekko makes the benignly wise and paternal businessman in *Goodbye Columbus* (who advised the story's protagonist that "to get by in business you've got to be a bit of a thief") look good in comparison.

Some important observers of business have seen things differently. The widely read "personal excellence" gurus Steven Covey and Tom Peters, for example, have pointed to the practical utility of moral virtues such as compassion, responsibility, fairness, and honesty. They suggest that virtue is part and parcel of the recipe for success, and that moral standards are not merely commendable choices but *necessary ingredients* for a thriving business career. This is a frequent theme in commencement addresses and other personal testimonials: virtuous behavior will advance a career in the long run by building trust and reputation, whereas ethical shortcomings will eventually derail a career. Business schools send similar messages by mandating courses in ethics for their students. Who's right—those who believe that morality and business are naturally opposed to one another or those who believe that the two are compatible? Those who believe that "nice guys finish last" or those who advocate "doing well by doing good"? Is the business world a den of thievery or a haven for upstanding citizens?

In this book, I show that a strong sense of moral purpose and ethical conviction not only promotes a business career but also provides a telling *advantage* in the quest to build a thriving enterprise. A sense of moral purpose is at the center of many business innovations. Morality is far more than a constraining force that keeps people upstanding and out of trouble. It is a fertile source of the imaginative ideas that inform and motivate enterprises, a wellspring of creative inspiration, a pillar of perseverance, far more than a mere restraint on illegitimate behavior. This is a different view of morality than one finds in a typical business ethics course. It is a broader and more inclusive concept, and, most important, it is more positive.

Morality in Business Reconsidered

Morality in business has multiple faces, each playing its own special role in ensuring business success. The most familiar face is known as "business ethics," correctly considered to be the prudent voice that warns us to stay out of trouble. When adhered to, such moral codes as "don't cheat, don't steal, don't bribe, don't discriminate, don't sexually harass your employees" work to rein in impulses that could be hazardous to one's business (and one's career) if left unchecked. In addition to legal and civil penalties that may result from being caught red-handed in an outright offense, there is the matter of one's reputation. It does no one in business good to become known as a shady character. Organizations too must guard their public images. As any good public relations firm knows, a clean ethical slate is a precious asset for any company, as valuable as an irreplaceable piece of property.

Another familiar way of acknowledging the moral dimension in business is through philanthropic giving. Many businesspeople donate to philanthropic causes, such as charity for the needy and support for education or the arts. Often this is done with an eye to one's reputation: a person, or a company, can try to build (or, in some cases, repair) an image of integrity through generous philanthropic giving. And for many who give, the impulse is genuine, stemming from a sense of social responsibility. As a rule, philanthropic giving comes *after* the business has made rich profit. It is not part and parcel of the profit making itself.

These first two dimensions of business morality—ethics and

philanthropic giving—are familiar because their benefits to self and society are so evident. It is clear to most people that unethical business practices need to be constrained because they place careers at risk, harm the public, and undermine business relationships. It is just as clear that charitable behavior not only improves the community but also elevates one's place in it. Both moral dimensions contribute directly to the enlightened interests of anyone who wishes to build an enduring business career.

But two other, less familiar, moral dimensions are also central to business success. One is a way of using moral purposes as a source of fruitful ideas, and the other is a way of collaborating based on principles of empathy, perspective-taking, and the Golden Rule. These dimensions contribute directly to the capacity for successful accomplishment in business; indeed, they are generative of most cutting-edge work. But they are not often noted (with some prominent exceptions), because few who rely on these moral dimensions trumpet them; in fact, people may not be fully aware of the role of these principles in their own success. These two dimensions are the elements of morality that are responsible for the proactive promotion of positive initiatives, in contrast to the negative avoidance of ethical breaches that we often think of when we use the term *moral conduct*.

A positive initiative may be as simple as an urge to serve customers better by bringing them a less expensive product, or it may be as complex as wanting to wire every neighborhood on earth for computing. There is a sense of purpose at the heart of every great business success. Of course, people in business have many other motives and inclinations too, including a desire to make lots of money, to prove oneself, to gain social status and control, to work on something interesting, to have fun, and so on. As I noted in the book's Introduction, I am not claiming pure moral motives. Rather, I am pointing out that a moral purpose always plays some role, because it is needed for creating and sustaining the innovation that achieves success.

The four roles of morality in business that I noted—the two familiar ways (protective and charitable) and the two less recognized

ways (proactive moral imagination and empathy-based relationships)—represent distinct but complementary means of moral
advantage. In this book, I devote a chapter to each dimension. I first
introduce the aspect of the moral imagination (in Chapter 3) and
follow that with empathy (Chapter 4), ethics (Chapter 5), and
finally philanthropy (Chapter 6). I have chosen this order to indicate
the developmental sequence through which morality in business
typically unfolds, as I explain next.

The Four Dimensions of Business Morality

As a shorthand, I call the four dimensions of business morality the
generative, empathic, restrictive, and *philanthropic* modes. *Generative*
morality hinges on the use of moral imagination to create innovative
initiatives that reflect noble purposes. *Empathic* morality hinges on the
use of perspective-taking and the Golden Rule to build strong collaborative relations with employees, partners, investors, clients, and customers. *Restrictive* morality hinges on the use of ethics to prevent damaging and disreputable practices. *Philanthropic* morality hinges on the
use of charitable giving to share part of one's profits with worthy
causes. Some distinctions among the four are drawn in Table 1.

    Generative morality arises from deep inner purposes and beliefs.
Not everyone feels such purposes and beliefs, or sees how to connect
them to their career choices. But those who do often find these core
beliefs to be a valuable source of inspiration in their work. Deep
purposes and beliefs provide the sparks of imagination that can give
birth to a new business concept. They also can provide a sense of
commitment that can sustain the concept during inevitable periods
of doubt, stress, and temporary reversals. They provide a reason to
go to the mat for an idea, a steel foundation for the persistence
always needed to implement any innovation. I place this dimension
first because it is the mode of morality that people tend to be most
in tune with when they first choose a career and set their goals.
People who enter business to make positive contributions to the
world (the "what" and "why" questions discussed in the Introduction) are motivated by purposes and beliefs that can form the basis
of a highly generative morality. The key to success, as I will show in

TABLE I. The Four Faces of Morality in Business

	Generative	*Empathic*	*Restrictive*	*Philanthropic*
Function	Inspiration	Collaboration	Protection	Promote worthy cause
Source	Deep beliefs	Perspective-taking	Traditional codes	Charitable impulse
Instrument	Imagination	Golden Rule	Conduct	Earned profits
Venue	Products, services	Relationships	Management	Outside institutions
Outcome	Innovation, sales	Trust, morale	Reputation, safety	Reputation, satisfaction

Chapter 3, is to nurture this fertile source of creative imagination rather than allowing it to fade away over the course of a career filled with compromise and burnout.

Empathic morality is an approach to business relationships that reflects the Golden Rule principle of treating others as you yourself would like to be treated. It fosters trust, collaboration, understanding, and communication. In Chapter 4, I will show the many productive uses of empathic morality in the business world.

Restrictive morality is the widely shared societal code of ethics that protects people from trouble, regulates their behavior according to the traditional norms that society demands, guards their reputation, and provides them with safety from legal attack. It is the mode of morality most strongly emphasized by business-school ethics courses and corporate ethics training. Important though such training can be, its effectiveness often suffers by taking ethics out of the context of the broad personal and social concerns that are included in the other three moral dimensions. In Chapter 5, I will present a more integrated—and more positive—approach to business ethics.

Philanthropic morality reflects a charitable impulse, donating a share of profits for altruistic ends. It requires the same sense of purpose, diligence, and humility that is required by the business success that brought the profits in the first place. When done properly, philanthropic morality reaps benefits beyond pure altruism, such as enhancing the reputation of the business leader and the company in the communities in which they operate. When done poorly, however, philanthropy causes more harm than good, damaging both the community and the donor's reputation. In Chapter 6, I discuss the challenges of using philanthropic morality to promote worthy causes.

Using the Four Moral Dimensions to Build a Rewarding Career

In our interviews with top business leaders, we found frequent mention of all four dimensions of business morality. The men and women differed in which of these aspects they personally emphasized, but there was virtually no disagreement about their importance. In the following four chapters, I illustrate how each dimension is used in a real business life, quoting some of the business leaders as they offer details about how they employed their moral convictions in the service of their work. For each chapter, I have selected cases that represent especially relevant examples of the moral dimension discussed therein. But the set of interviews as a whole contains many other cases that I could have used to illustrate the same points, because all of the business leaders in our study expressed commitment to these moral modes.

Approximately two-thirds of the business leaders reported use of generative morality, in the sense of drawing on beliefs and purposes for inspiration. Many talked about how they used their moral imaginations to produce innovative business concepts, and to muster the persistence and commitment needed for sticking with a new idea despite skepticism and the risk of the unknown. Some said they actively train their minds to nurture this kind of moral creativity.

Many interviewees reported relying on religious or spiritual faith to spur creative inspiration and sustain their mental discipline, a characteristic not typically evident among business leaders because they tend to keep their faith private to avoid being perceived as imposing their own religious beliefs on employees. In our study, however, more than 90 percent of the people interviewed expressed a devout spiritual or religious faith of some kind. Few executives try to use their businesses to advocate for a particular religious or spiritual doctrine. Rather, they take their own inspiration and commitments from their faith, and keep it to themselves in their day-to-day business operations.

I first realized the power of generative morality a few years ago when I met with Sir John Templeton, the legendary business leader to whom I have dedicated this book. It was clear to me that Templeton's business accomplishments reflected a deeper sense of purpose, a purpose closely linked to his spiritual beliefs. For him, it was faith that fueled his moral imagination. Connecting the dots, I could see that this had been the primary wellspring of Templeton's daring and creative path to success.

When Templeton was active in business, he was an investment manager who gained international renown, a vast fortune, and a British knighthood for his distinguished service to the Crown. He was the first investment manager to create a global family of mutual funds. As early as the 1930s, before the advent of the personal computer or international jet travel, Templeton found economic value in places where few Western investors had thought to look—in Asia, the Middle East, Australia, even remote parts of Africa. The value was there. The Templeton funds grew from a one-room operation over a local police station into a multibillion-dollar corporation. The way that Templeton came up with this concept reveals how business leaders use generative morality as a source of innovative business concepts.

What gave him the vision to explore global investing and the fortitude to gamble in such little-known territories? One answer to this (not the only one, but a key piece of the puzzle) lies in Templeton's commitment to his particular faith. He devoutly believes in the love of all humanity, without discrimination of any sort. As a young man, Templeton first considered becoming a minister, but while in college he decided that his gifts were in financial analysis and that he could best serve God and humanity in this way. (He told me that his only regret is that he did not start his mutual funds earlier "because I would have served many more people.")

Central to Templeton's belief is the idea that all people are "only the tiniest part of God." Therefore, "each of us should try to love every human being without *any* exceptions, and not just a little bit, but unlimited love for every human being with absolutely no exceptions." Separating people by tribe, race, club, or nation is "probably not as healthy" as thinking of all humanity as one. Templeton is not a fan of narrow, overly chauvinistic sentiments that divide people. His purpose of celebrating the infinite worth of all people, and his belief in the essential unity of humanity, led him directly to the notion of global mutual finds. Although this notion has become commonplace in the financial world by now, it was radical and untested when Templeton first introduced it. Who, after all, could imagine that companies in strange, faraway places might be worth investing in? But the risks that he took on his faith's behalf were richly rewarded.

Templeton never used his companies to proselytize for his particular faith. He did not expect his employees or his customers to join his own church. What he *did* do was express his vision by founding a truly international, boundary-crossing approach to investing, an approach that seemed risky and audacious at the time but that ultimately proved brilliantly successful. Material success followed from Templeton's spiritual inspiration in ways that would be hard to trace without knowing his innermost sense of purpose.

A powerful concept lies at the heart of every successful business. In the most spectacular cases, the new business concept—a car in every garage, airplane travel for the masses, a computer on every desk—transforms the way people conduct their lives. How do businessmen and -women come up with powerful new ideas? Where do they get the nerve to commit themselves to an unproven idea when people who seem to know better say that they are crazy? Where does the spirit of innovation come from, and the mettle required to venture down a new road? Templeton gave me my first inkling of where successful businesspeople find this kind of inspiration and strength.

The other business leaders whom I interviewed filled in the rest of the story. In Chapter 3, I will present some further examples of the moral imagination at work.

Once a concept is born out of an inspiring sense of purpose, it must be communicated to those necessary to make the concept a reality: partners and investors, coworkers and employees, clients and customers. The communication must keep the company focused on the concept and see that it is executed with conviction. Such communication rests on the trust and respect of all those who must buy into the concept. Building trusting relationships among disparate groups of people is a serious accomplishment in itself, because each group—whether partners, employees, investors, or customers—has its own special interests at stake. The only way to get all of these people to trust what a leader is saying is to gain a reputation for decency and honesty in one's dealings with others.

Among the business leaders we interviewed, we found that many look to the age-old principle of the Golden Rule as their way to ensure that their behavior conforms to such standards as decency and honesty. At the heart of the Golden Rule is empathy, the sense that everyone shares in one another's joys and pains and therefore that everyone must care about the conditions in which others find themselves. In our study, almost all of the men and women expressed an active commitment to building trusting relationships through empathic understanding and other principles consistent with the Golden Rule. Without prompting, more than one-fourth invoked the Golden Rule itself to explain how they manage relations with partners, clients, and employees.

Closely tied to empathy is the capacity to take the perspective of the other, to "step inside another person's shoes." This capacity can be cultivated to great effect in one's business relationships. In Chapter 4, I will present examples of how businesspeople employ empathy, perspective-taking, and the Golden Rule to cultivate the productive and trusting relations that they must build with colleagues, employees, and customers.

What applies within companies also applies among companies. In addition to fostering trusting communication within their own companies, business leaders today say that they must establish good collaborative relations *across* organizations, even in cases where those organizations have a fundamentally competitive relationship with one another. Some interviewees in the high-tech corridors of Silicon Valley and Boston, for example, called this "co-opetition," although others outside of those regions spurn this term as New Age jargon. Yet by whatever name this trend is called, most try to practice it, because they believe that in today's ever-shifting business world, this kind of cross-company teamwork provides a decisive advantage, an advantage that hinges on a leader's reputation for decent conduct and trustworthiness.

Beyond empathy, stringent ethical conduct—what I have called *restrictive morality*—is a key element in a reputation for trustworthiness. More than four-fifths of the business leaders in our study placed an extremely high priority on restrictive morality. Their commitment revolved around such values as resistance to corruption and refusal to cut corners in truthfulness, fairness, and respect for the law. These values guided their relations with partners, employees, customers, competitors, and society at large. The interviewees reported that these values had enabled them to reject frequent pressures to give (or take) bribes, to put out deceitful public information, to renege on contracts, to manipulate share prices, to cover up defective products, to steal other people's inventions, to cheat vendors or customers by unfair pricing, or to harm their communities through irresponsible environmental policies—any of which could spell trouble if practiced and then revealed.

This ethical sense also helped these business leaders establish dependable relations with colleagues and competitors. They see this as an urgent challenge in today's fluid marketplace. Because of globalization, technological innovation, and conglomeration, companies rise and disappear quickly. Jobs are created and lost overnight, and workers move on the instant they spot a new opportunity. What does this mean for working relationships within a company, including the bonds between leader and staff? Are traditional notions such as loyalty still useful, or even viable? Is teamwork possible among people who may become competitors by the time of the next paycheck? The business leaders in our study used ethical principles to create a spirit of cooperation in their intensely competitive environments.

Finally, philanthropic morality is a widely followed path of public service in the business world, as four-fifths of the business leaders in our study subscribed to such a practice. Philanthropy enables business leaders to define relations with the broader community in ways that yield benefits for both the community and the company, especially providing the company with compelling and legitimate public relations material. In certain cases, philanthropy can feed back to a business's founding mission, thus serving the generative function as well as the community-relations one. For example, a computer company that donates equipment to schools not only aids the worthy cause of education but also expands its future market by enlarging its consumer base and building brand recognition within it.

Although philanthropy rightly occupies an honored place among the four dimensions of business morality, it is not as certain a means to doing good as it may first appear. Believe it or not, simply giving away a bunch of money does not always improve the lot of those who receive it, as many philanthropists discover, to their regret. The same moral qualities that lead to success in business— purpose, insight, empathy, humility, honesty, trustworthiness—are also required for effective philanthropy. For this reason, among many others, philanthropy should never be seen as a sure-fire salvation for a corrupt and ruthless business career. Although careful philanthropy can bring many good things to the world, it is neither redemptive nor certain. Andrew Carnegie once said that it is harder to give money away well than to make it.

The Development of Moral Identity

The four dimensions of morality that I just described each serve an important function (outlined earlier in Table 1). In an operational sense, there is a time and a place for each one, because the moralities operate differently, solve distinct kinds of problems, and produce different sorts of results. But in a personal sense, these four dimensions develop together, as part of the person's never-ending quest to build an admirable character.

This is not to say, in reality, that anyone ever manages to act perfectly with respect to all four moral dimensions. Indeed, the reason that one's quest for character is never-ending is that everyone is far from perfect, and even the most reputable people will behave inconsistently at times. These dimensions themselves can stand in conflict, as when a creative idea that reflects a driving purpose (an example of generative morality) is misrepresented to best market the idea (a restrictive morality breach). Or any one of the moralities may be neglected for periods of time, as when a rising business leader decides that the time for philanthropic giving has not yet come.

In the long run, all four moral dimensions contribute to a full life in business, and a person fully armed has an enduring moral advantage. When integrated in a person's character, the four enhance and reinforce one another. The way that this happens in the course of development is by forging a strong *moral identity*. This process usually begins when young, often as early as adolescence (although it is never too late for someone to start), and it continues throughout life. Identity is a person's sense of who he or she is, and who he or she would like to become.[3] Moral identity is the part that revolves around the person's moral convictions—the sense that I am honest, compassionate, responsible, fair, and trustworthy, and that these are important defining features of who I am and what I want to be like.

The development of moral identity begins with the discovery of what convictions most matter to you. (This is what Robert Greenleaf meant by the "act of self-discovery" first mentioned in Chapter 1.) These convictions, once fully realized, directly lead to purposes to which you can dedicate yourself. For example, if you have a conviction that people have a right to food and shelter, you might dedicate yourself to purposes that provide these essential commodities to the poor. Of course, there are any number of ways that you might go about doing this, including new ways that others haven't thought of. When you dream up new ways of accomplishing a moral purpose, you are using your moral imagination, or engaging in an act of generative morality. In this sense, the drive to accomplish a moral purpose is the trigger for both the formation of moral identity and the acts of creation that generate new solutions to moral problems.

Once convictions are found and purposes established, they need to be pursued in a manner true to the moral nature of the conviction. Killing all poor people would not be a moral solution to eradicating poverty. The *means* of the act must be just as moral as the *ends*. No matter how lofty our goals, they have little moral worth unless we pursue them with decency, honesty, compassion, and respect. For this reason, developing the capacity (and the will) to act empathically and ethically is critical to the forging of a strong moral identity. Empathy and ethics ensure that moral purposes will be pursued by moral means. In the case of empathy, we follow moral means out of concern for the other, as expressed by the Golden Rule. In the case of ethics, we follow moral means out of conformity to the codes of society. The two together create a powerful incentive to act in an upstanding manner.

Capping the development of moral identity is the sense of the self as a responsible citizen in one's community and society. This sense of citizenship develops gradually over the adult years, as a person takes on responsible social roles such as worker, spouse, parent, and active community member. In business, a prime way to express a sense of responsible citizenship in the broader society is through philanthropy. Business leaders usually wait to begin their philanthropic efforts until after they have established their businesses, and they accelerate them only when profitability grows. But, as I noted previously, even though philanthropy tends to grow later in life, it draws on the same moral convictions and virtues used in the earlier achievement of business success. In this sense, philanthropic morality is linked to all other components of a person's developing moral identity.

Figure 1 indicates the ordering of the four dimensions of business morality in the course of a person's development of moral identity. The logic of the pyramid shape is that the direction of development (beginning with purpose and moving up through the empathic, restrictive, and philanthropic moralities) also reveals the practical relationship of the moralities to one another in the business

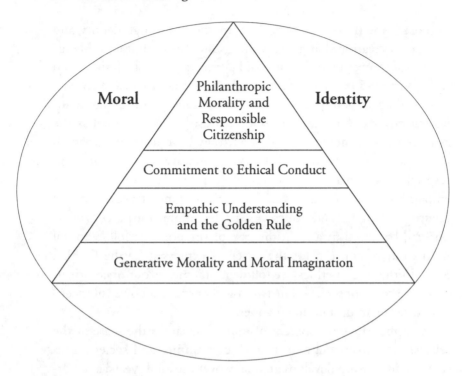

Figure 1. The Pyramid of Business Moralities

world. Although each moral dimension plays an important role in itself, some are more fundamental than others in the sense that they drive and sustain the others. The foundation of business success is a sense of moral purpose (at the bottom of the pyramid). Without purpose, a person tends to see the other dimensions of morality merely as rules and proscriptions: they are to be followed when necessary (or convenient), but they do not have a compelling rationale of their own. A lack of purpose will always put the other moral dimensions on shaky ground. Only when shored up by a constant focus on purpose can they be reliably counted on.

Moving up the pyramid, all dimensions of moral action draw on prior dimensions for their meaning and sustenance. Restrictive morality, for example, can be no more than a negative force—and consequently a weak one—without a concern for purpose, fairness, and compassion. When based on an awareness of these fundamental moral concerns, the restrictive ethical codes that constrain illegitimate behavior come naturally, because they feel internally generated rather than externally imposed. Similarly, philanthropy can be an empty shell, possibly doing more harm than good, unless it is based on a sense of moral purpose and conducted in an empathic and ethical manner.

Surrounding the four moral dimensions in Figure 1 is moral identity, from which all moral commitment springs. As a rule, a person acquires the elements of moral identity in the same order as indicated by the direction of the pyramid, with purpose coming first (often in late adolescence), followed by commitments to empathic understanding, ethics, and philanthropy (or other acts of responsible citizenship). But the order is not a rigid one, and there is always interaction among the moral dimensions as they develop. They play in to one another, growing organically as they feed the person's moral identity. In the end, in the best cases, the four dimensions become fully integrated, as part of a mature personality. This integration is what I refer to as "integrity," the heart and soul of moral character.

The Importance of Moral Identity in Business and in Life

People in business differ enormously in how central their moral concerns are to their senses of who they are and who they want to be. For some, moral convictions largely define who they are. For others, material concerns (how much money they have, how powerful they happen to be, and so on) are far more central. It is the former who are most likely to live a life of moral integrity.

Our studies have found that a person's moral identity is the best predictor of the person's commitment to moral action, because it determines not merely what the person considers to be the right course of action but also why a person would decide that "I myself must take this course." For example, most persons will express the belief that allowing others to starve is morally wrong, but only some of these people will conclude that they *themselves* must do something to prevent this in a particular circumstance, such as a famine in Africa. Moral identity engenders a sense of personal responsibility for taking action: it provides a powerful incentive for conduct, because it triggers a motive to act in accordance with one's conception of one's ideal self. Moral judgment alone cannot provide this motive: it is only when people conceive of themselves, and their life goals, in moral terms that they acquire a strong propensity to act according to their moral judgments. As one psychologist writes, "If a person sees a value or a way of life as essential to their identity, then they feel that they ought to act accordingly."[4]

In the book *Some Do Care*, Anne Colby and I found that the moral exemplars whom we studied were convinced that the work that they were doing fulfilled both their personal *and* moral goals.[5] Because their work was driven by personal and moral motives, these exemplars were able to sustain the hard, year-after-year commitments that enabled them to tackle tough, seemingly impossible problems and to accomplish marked results. In other words, they demonstrated high degrees of moral identity, signaled by a strong integration between the self and moral concerns.[6] At the same time, these subjects did not demonstrate elevated moral reasoning on our standard moral judgment measures. We concluded that sustained moral commitment requires a strong moral identity rather than sophisticated reasoning abilities. That is, "people who define themselves in terms of their moral goals are likely to see moral problems in everyday events, and they are also likely to see themselves as necessarily implicated in these problems. From there it is a small step to taking responsibility for the solution."[7]

Moral identity in business means defining the self in a way that includes not only one's work-related skills and interests but also one's sense of moral purpose for one's work, one's sense of ethical restrictions, and one's responsibility to one's community. In our study of two hundred successful professionals working in science and the news media, Howard Gardner, Mihaly Csikszentmihalyi, and I found that those who consistently upheld the loftiest traditions of their professions had strong senses of moral identity.[8] Some were motivated to conduct their work in a moral manner by always want-ing to pass "the mirror test" when they returned home from work each day.

Moral identity provides a sense of personal responsibility for making moral choices. Over the course of human development, when a person makes moral choices regularly, they become habitual: a child who has learned to be honest does not need to decide whether to lie, cheat, or steal every time the chance arises. In normal circumstances, the honest behavior comes naturally—or, to use a more accurate idiom, by second nature. That is, through a system of acquired action the behavior becomes habitual. Well-established moral habits are commonly known as virtues, which in turn form the behavioral basis of moral character.[9]

"If you do the right thing," said Mike Hackworth, the founder and CEO of Cirrus Logic and Aspirian, two enormously profitable Silicon Valley technology companies, "you're not going to be embar-rassed, it's not going to come back on you. I always keep in mind that I don't want to do anything that I wouldn't want my mother to read about in the newspaper. Actually, what she said to me, and it imparted on me an ethic, 'You don't want to do anything that, if you decide to run for president, they would publish it in a newspaper later on.'" Many others whom we interviewed expressed the same sentiments in different words: "I care about the kind of person I am." "I need to be able to look in the mirror and like what I see." And, "At the end of the day, what counts is your integrity, your rep-utation for good work, your word, your honor"—signs of one's moral identity.

People who function at the highest levels, maximizing all their potentials, strive for a unity in the self among personal and moral concerns. Although absolute unity is rarely achieved (other than by moral exemplars with extraordinary degrees of moral commitment), anyone can approach this ideal over time. Cultivating a moral iden-tity—the sense that moral concerns play a key role in determining who I am and who I want to be—is the psychological means to this end. People who have gained enduring success in their business and community lives reflect this sense. They pay attention to the "inner voice" that provides them with a moral compass, and they learn to guide their conduct according to the virtues and principles that flow from their moral identities. It is a lifelong quest.

The consequences of that quest begin with the self but go far beyond it. The character of any organization is determined by the character of the men and women who work in it. If the organization is to avoid ethical pitfalls, acquire an admirable reputation, and serve its customers in an innovative and valuable manner, the "inner voices" of those men and women must steer them in the right direction.

Moral identity is as important on the organizational level as on the personal level. When the two levels are in synch, with a focused sense of moral purpose and a clear ethical compass to guide them, the incentives of the organization become well aligned with the workers' highest aspirations. When they are out of synch, however, workers are discouraged from making the right choices and rewarded for the wrong behavior. Every business leader's charge is to make sure that his or her organization does not just profess an ethical code, but that it reflects a genuine sense of moral identity in its approach to clients, customers, employees, and all the other stakeholders.

This should also be the charge of ethics training in business schools and other educational settings (such as midcareer workshops). Unfortunately, too often it is not. Most ethical training in business fails to engage students in the profound questions of how workers and organizations can build strong moral identities. Most ethics courses tend to dwell on philosophical dilemmas and hypothetical scenarios, which students may experience more as problems in logic than in personal character development. At times, notorious cases of scandals are used to illustrate the real-life dangers of fraud, but even then, the world is cast in stark terms of good and evil, and the solution offered is a set of rules, mostly legal, by which students are implored to abide.

Predictably, this odd combination of philosophical game-playing and scary sermonizing leaves students cold. Anyone who hangs around a business school knows that few students take their mandated ethics courses seriously: they attend to fulfill the requirement and then blow it off without much further thought. In fact, one recent study of almost two thousand graduates from thirteen top business schools found that "B-School education not only fails to improve the moral character of its students, it actually weakens it."[10] Noting that study and his own observations of programs at Harvard and elsewhere, sociologist Amitai Etzioni concludes: "Business schools—the training grounds for corporate tycoons—have been forced to face the fact that they have failed to produce honest brokers."[11]

The heart of the matter, still unexplored in almost all business schools, is how people in business can develop the kind of all-consuming sense of purpose that fires their imaginations and guides their every choice. B-school ethics courses have narrowly confined themselves to what I call "restrictive morality" and have lacked the vision to engage with the larger issues of moral identity and character development. As I have discussed earlier in this chapter, restrictive morality is essential but incomplete. It does not in itself provide a sufficient foundation for purpose, empathy, or success. Alone, it is wholly negative and uninspiring: no wonder students let it pass through one ear and out the other.

There is a recent movement in the social sciences called "positive psychology."[12] It is an approach that tries to capture the positive inner forces that move people, rather than the fears and baser drives that Freud and other past luminaries of the field emphasized. Although it is still young, the positive psychology movement is attracting notable attention from those who believe that people, when given the chance, will dedicate themselves to things that inspire them, and only in doing so will they find real satisfaction and happiness.[13]

In the framework presented in this chapter, the key is the whole pyramid. No single dimension suffices to forge a moral identity in business: they all must be pursued together, as a piece. It is not always possible for anyone—even the highest-minded person—to accomplish this: as I stressed in the Introduction, mixed motives and imperfections are part of every life story. People who succeed do the best they can, making as few compromises as possible. Over the long haul, by sustaining their quests, their moral identities strengthen and they grow in integrity. Such people build lives of satisfaction for themselves and service for the many who benefit from their achievements. I now turn to some of these people.

3 Generative Morality: Acts of Creation

In business as in life, the moral imagination is a fertile source of creative ideas. Of course it is not our only source of creative ideas—almost any flight of fancy can lead somewhere if we are prepared to follow it up properly—but the moral imagination is a source that has exceptional staying power. Backed up by our deepest beliefs, an idea generated by moral imaginings cannot easily be beaten down. We go to the mat for it, amid doubts and criticism. We take risks that otherwise might seem unbearable, because we have faith in the fundamental worthiness of the idea. In the face of daunting skepticism, this kind of persistence is exactly what is needed to see a bold new concept to fruition.

Both entrepreneurs and managers draw creative new ideas from their moral imaginations, the generative dimension of business morality. As with all of the moral dimensions, the consistent use of generative morality can give companies unmatchable advantages in the marketplace. Entrepreneurs generate creative ideas that help develop better products and services; managers generate ideas that help them build stronger organizations. And many business leaders wear entrepreneurial and managerial hats, using their moral creativity both to generate new concepts for products and services and to invent new solutions to tough personnel problems. In this chapter, I discuss the uniquely valuable contributions of moral imagination for both these business uses.

What Is the Moral Imagination and How Does It Work?

Much of our mental life is ruled by habits, routines, and "scripts" that we learn and fix in memory. When we sit down in a restaurant, we don't need to figure out what a menu is or how to get the waiter to bring food; we just rely on what we know from past experience. Perhaps 90 percent of our thought processes—perceptions, judgments, reactions, choices—derive directly from ways of knowing that have become habitual and more or less automatic. There are differences among people in this regard—some people rely more than others on fixed mental habits in responding to events—but even the most original and creative people experience most of life through stable thought patterns that have been gradually built over time.

This is usually a good thing: when a person's mental reactions are unpredictable and in constant flux, we fear for the person's sanity. But there are some breaks in the routine that are welcome, representing real progress over what was known before. These creative breaks are all the more remarkable when viewed in the context of the mental system's normally high degree of stability.

The mental system is self-protective and resistant to change, with a natural—and adaptive—aversion to too much disruption and distraction. Consequently, the stakes are high for any attempt to introduce genuinely new ideas into the system. This means that the *source* of such ideas, if the ideas are to be taken seriously and acted on, must be something in which the person has faith. The great traditions of human culture—science, religion, art, philosophy—offer sources of support for new ideas that inspire just this kind of faith.

Moral imagination is the capacity to generate creative new ideas that spring from one's moral sense. Morality itself is a great tradition of human culture, although it is by no means a stand-alone tradition: it overlaps with all of the other dimensions in some way. There is a morality of science (truth-seeking and other ethical concerns), a morality of art (truth and responsibility), and of course both religion and philosophy concern themselves with the definition and meaning of morality. Morality is also a matter of intuition and feeling. Studies of moral development reveal that even young infants experience moral emotions such as empathy, shame, and guilt, and that these natural inclinations play a key role in one's moral conduct all through life.[1]

In generating new ideas, the moral imagination draws on any and all of these sources of moral tradition, insight, intuition, and feeling. To be "imaginative" generally means having a rich fantasy life. We value this capacity for many reasons, including its contribution to playfulness and recreation. But to be imaginative in the service of one's work requires a special sort of creativity, a creativity grounded in a sense of reality and constrained by a sense of discipline. The flight of fancy must have a purpose that it springs from and returns to if it is to accomplish something worthwhile. Ensuring the "return flight" is the job of mental discipline, but there can be nothing to return to without an original sense of galvanizing purpose.

In the introductory chapter of this book, I discussed the importance of purpose in a business life. Purpose is at the heart of generative morality, an enabler of the creativity that marks distinguished accomplishments and successful careers. It provides food for the moral imagination. Now there are many kinds of purpose that inspire people in business, and only some of these are moral in nature. Most accomplishments are produced by mixed motives, as I noted in the Introduction, and the drive to make money is always part of the mix. But no mind ever dreamed up a winning new concept for a business product or service by dwelling on moneymaking alone. At some point, there must be a focus on the product or service itself. The more intense and sustained the focus, the more likely it is that the new concept will be original, sound, workable, and of recognized value to consumers.

This kind of purpose-driven focus offers an advantage to businesses of every type, no matter how small or ordinary. An auto-repair shop with mechanics who believe in their work will come up with more creative solutions for broken cars than one with mechanics who merely put in their time. As one reviewer of this book manuscript wrote about her own dedicated mechanic, "Because of my mechanic's pride and passion in his work, he may notice things about my car that others would overlook, or he may take extra time to train his junior mechanics to exacting standards, or he may implement innovative new practices."[2]

Moral imagination creates this kind of intense and sustained focus. It is not the only means to this end—for example, scientific and aesthetic imagination work in much the same way—but it is the mental tool among all the others that has the greatest reach and staying power. Its domain is the entire range of human needs that every entrepreneur thirsts to fill. An idea formed through moral imagination engenders a special kind of commitment, because it is an idea that reflects the deepest beliefs of the person who thought it up. So, for example, when Sir John Templeton turned his belief in the universality of human talent into a family of global mutual funds, as I described in Chapter 2, he was not about to give up on the idea after a few reversals. He was a believer, highly resistant to discouragement.

The business leaders interviewed for this book used their moral imaginations in a variety of ways. For some, it was a matter of directly extrapolating a new business concept from a moral (and often spiritual) worldview. For others, it was a sensitivity to what consumers need and a determination to respond effectively to that. For still others, it was a commitment to a caring and ethical manner of doing business that required inventive approaches to organizing employees. And for a few, it was all of the above. Examining a number of these cases provides a concrete sense of how moral imagination works in all its varieties.

Gloria Falla

As vice president for design at Sara Lee Branded Apparel, Gloria Falla is in charge of seeing to it that the lingerie that Playtex sells, which millions of women around the world wear, is both beautiful and comfortable. In her executive role, Falla heads up a team of

Gloria Falla

fashion designers, expert fitters, tailors, and fashion consultants. And as a designer herself, she creates many of the concepts that become new lines of intimate wear.

I begin here with Falla not because of the glamour associated with her work—indeed, although the product is glamorous, the process of creating stylish lingerie appears as prosaic as any other task—but rather because she articulated so clearly the special attitudes and dispositions of all the successful men and women with whom we spoke. Falla's passion for her work, her sense of purpose, the spiritual source of her inspiration, her devotion to her colleagues, and her commitment to ethical behavior may be extraordinary in the overall scheme of things (unfortunately), but they are commonplace among those who find both meaning *and* success in their work.

The morning that I spoke with Falla, her office was humming from the reverberations of a major fashion show that it had just put on. The office walls glowed with pictures of models wearing the latest in underwear fashions. Any notions I had about the simplicity of designing intimate apparel quickly vanished when I met Falla and listened to her speak about her work. Creating a bra, she said, "is almost like building a bridge":

> You have to hold these things up! . . . I know that a bra has a function, you know, like a car. But how do you camouflage the mechanics of a car to be beautiful and functional at the same

time? So that's what I try to do in the product that I design. Make it beautiful, but functional, because it is the first thing you put on in the morning. It's got to be comfortable enough, and pretty enough, that you forget that you have it on. So, to me, it's just great, I love doing what I do. I never get tired. I could be here forever. And there are times when I say to myself, "I'm going home at 4:30," and it's 6:30 and I'm still sitting here, right? So, I never, never mind the time that I put into this because it never seems like work.

I treat all my jobs as if the company was my own, because I give it 110 percent all the time. And I've had wonderful jobs, and worked in different companies, and I've always done something unique with each company, and learned a great deal, and evolved. For instance, when I worked at Lily of France, I was the first designer in the industry to create a bra with a stretch lace back—something we named Lace Embrace. For this I won the 1984 Dallas Fashion Award for innovation. I believe, as a designer, I should strive for innovation and pragmatism on each garment that I create.

This enthusiastic statement of purpose—even to the point of devotion—comes from a woman who was brought to the United States at age nine as a refugee from Cuba, speaking almost no English and hating the strange northern climate with its early dark evenings. But Falla adapted rapidly. She worked hard in school, and she found her special love during the after-school hours: "I would come home from school, and make myself a dress to wear the next day. And I would do [special] things. I remember making a blouse that had lacing in the back, and now lacing is in fashion. So, you see, I was ahead of my time and creative way back then! It was a question of putting my talent to use where I could be the most creative and effective."

Falla discovered her creative niche early, guided by the advice of a professor at the Fashion Institute of Technology in New York. The advice was both well given and well taken. One of the characteristics of successful businesspeople is their lifelong receptivity to guidance from those whom they admire: "When I started at school, I remember one of my professors said, 'Gloria, if you want to be an evening wear designer, there are a lot of evening gowns that have built-in bras, and you may want to take the course in foundations.' So I did. And I loved it. And I never went back to evening wear. I thought this was so exciting because not only could I be creative, but technical as well. So I've always liked the challenge of combining creative and technical design."

Although Falla enjoys the technical parts of her work, the real thrill, she said, is in creating something new, beautiful, and useful. She can hardly be contained when she talks about a new product: "I wanted to do something unique, technology-wise, and beautiful. I saw a pretty Playtex bra with a unique performance feature and thought, 'Here's a company that I would love to work for. A company that would encourage me to use all of my talents, both creative and technical.' So, that's what I try to do—I enhance people's figures, I lift their spirits as well as their bodies."

With her mission always clear in her mind, Falla searches for new ways of achieving it. This requires creativity, imagination, and, above all, focus. The best ideas often come at unexpected times, serendipitously, as part of a constant process of mental exploration and experimentation. It is a highly generative process, productive and energetic, motivated by a deep belief in the value of one's work. Although this process requires extraordinary amounts of effort and attention, it does not feel hard or burdensome. Rather, it feels absorbing, inspiring, pleasurable—much like engaging in a thrilling recreational activity. (My colleague Mihaly Csikszentmihalyi uses the term *flow* to describe these kinds of creative, high-energy states.[3])

Many of the businesspeople profiled in this book describe their own work experience in similar ways. Falla spoke for many of them when she told me: "I'm always thinking, always, always, always. I'm looking at magazines, movies, people on the street, and I can get inspiration anywhere. I can be in church, and think of something. I wake up during the night and jot down ideas, and say, 'I've got to do this.' Inspiration can happen anywhere at any time. It doesn't have a set time."

It was no accident that Falla mentioned "church" when she spoke about where she gets new ideas. For her, devout religious faith offers a crucial source of inspiration for her creativity. This is not as unusual as it may sound. As mentioned in previous chapters, in our study we found that religious faith was strongly associated both with ethical *and* creative work in business. The relation between belief and ethics may seem obvious, since all major religions promote rigorous ethical codes. But what may be less obvious is the way that many business leaders draw creative inspiration from their religious beliefs. Their faith imbues their work with a sense of purpose that energizes their imaginations and enables them to take the risks necessary to explore new and unknown directions. These business leaders generally keep their faith to themselves, exerting care not to use their positions to proselytize for their own particular beliefs. Falla was typical of many when she described the personal benefits of her faith: "I always think that I got my creative talent from God and that He's always been very generous to me. I always thank God, because I feel I've been able to do all these things because I was given a great talent; I was able to go to school, expand and learn."

Falla also credits the people she has worked with, including some key mentors, for further expanding that talent. In turn, she "spreads the joy," not through proselytizing but through sharing her expertise and enthusiasm with those working underneath her: "I've been very lucky that I've worked with some very talented and generous people that I've been able to learn a lot from. And now, of course, I try to do the same. I try to give back and teach. The designers that I work with see and hear the things that I do and how I do them, so that we spread the joy."

Ethical behavior—honesty, fairness, adherence to the common moral codes that make up one's social contract—is the foundation of an honorable life in business. In its absence, things fall apart— not always immediately, but eventually. If anybody needed a reminder of this (and, unfortunately, people often do because the pressures of competition and ambition have a way of squeezing ethics out of one's consciousness during eventful times), the corporate catastrophes of the early twenty-first century should have shaken them out of their stupor. For business leaders such as Falla, however, ethics is an intrinsic part of work, inseparable from all the other tasks and responsibilities. A commitment to ethical behavior seems natural and inevitable to such leaders, impossible to ignore because this is an essential part of who they are. It is a defining element of their moral identities.

Falla traces the incorporation of ethics into her sense of self back to her early childhood, and she credits her religious faith for helping to sustain it: "I think honesty is the most important thing. Because I remember my mother saying, 'You know, you should never lie, because you can always get caught. And, at the end of the day, God knows what you're doing. So, who are you going to hide from?' . . . and I also think, first and foremost, that respect is very important. And I treat all of my coworkers with respect, regardless of their position or their age. And I treat them the way that I would want them to treat me."

Here Falla implicitly alludes to the Golden Rule as a touchstone for her ethical behavior, as did many of the leaders we interviewed. In the minds of many successful businesspeople, the idea of treating others—whether partners, clients, customers, or subordinates—as they themselves expect to be treated set a binding standard for their behavior. They realized that the Golden Rule serves to both demand and provide a spirit of common decency in their workplaces.

Unlike Falla, however, not all of the people we interviewed traced their ethical commitments to early childhood: some came to their values relatively late in life, perhaps as a consequence of a close relationship with a respected mentor, or perhaps because of a revealing and memorable experience, sometimes negative in nature. Nor did everyone credit a religious faith with sustaining their ethical behavior under pressure—although, as I have noted, the degree of religiosity among these business leaders went far beyond my expectations. But, like Falla, *all* saw ethics as so much a part of how one conducts one's business that it was not even perceived as a matter of choice. That is, there was little sense of agonizing over whether to do the right thing versus cutting corners. That choice had been made long ago by our leaders, and now the ethical behavior is almost automatic.

Living the Golden Rule promotes not only ethical behavior but also humility. I have a lot to say in this book about humility. Of course, it is an admirable virtue that has been celebrated at least since biblical times. But beyond that, humility serves many psychological functions that help a person thrive intellectually and emotionally. Humility promotes an open-mindedness that enables us to continue learning throughout life. It provides us with a healthy perspective on our importance in the scheme of things. And, in an interpersonal sense, it enables us to build a sense of teamwork with our colleagues.

Falla refers to this last function when she describes how she never lets herself act or feel that she is better than her subordinates: "If our meeting room is a mess, I say, 'Guys, we've got to clean.' And the first one that gets the sponge out is me! And I do it because I always want to let them know that we're all the same. . . . We all pitch in and do it the same way. I want everyone to feel that we are a team even though we have different titles. I don't want them to ever feel that, just because I sit here, that I'm better than they are. Because, at the end of the day, I'm not."

Another occasion that Falla describes reveals her abiding determination to maintain her humility in the face of a constant onslaught of executive perks. To achieve this requires attention to detail and the inadvertent messages that small, overlooked signals can send: "For example, the designers and I went to a luncheon recently and when it was over, I didn't want them [her design team] to think that I was going to have a car service to take me home and they wouldn't. So I got cars for all of us, because at the end of the day, I don't want them to think, 'Well, she's the boss, and she's the only one to have a car to go home.' So, lo and behold, wouldn't you know it, my car comes first. . . . I felt like two cents because we couldn't switch cars. I immediately called the car service to confirm that the other car would be there soon because [the dispatcher] probably thought, 'She's the boss, she gets the (first) car,' and that's the last thing I wanted the designers to think. I have been in similar situations, and I've seen people do a lot of things that I said, 'God, I will never, ever do that.'"

It may be difficult for those who have not been exposed to the highest rungs on American corporate ladders to appreciate the constant drumbeat of temptations to feel superior to other mortals. The power can appear absolute at times. Tom Wolfe's phrase "masters of the universe" captures the psychological reality, if not, as his ironic tale indicated, the ultimate reality. All throughout a corporation, workers compete in a mad scramble to reinforce the executive's sense that he or she deserves plush privileges of every imaginable kind.

Another of our interviewees, Glen Hiner, who later became the CEO of a large building-supply company, told me about a revealing incident that occurred while he was a vice president and general manager at GE:

> One of the lessons of leadership that I was able to learn rather early on in my career has to do with the use of power. I think a lot of leaders don't understand the power that comes with the position and how to use that power, or how power might be used incorrectly.
>
> I had just been made a vice president of the company, and had just moved from Europe back to our U.S. headquarters, and on the first or second day on the job, I walked in early in the morning, and the maintenance people had just finished painting a wall. And I casually walked over to the maintenance supervisor who was standing there, and I said, "Gee what a nice wall, but it's too bad that you didn't paint it light blue. But we'll do that next time." The following morning, when I walked to work in the building, the wall was light blue. And I never forgot that. It made me very cautious and very careful in recognizing the authority and power that I had in my position, and how to utilize it and how not to use it.

Executives with a less-than-secure sense of who they are, and those who have not learned to appreciate the personal and social benefits offered by the virtue of humility, may be persuaded that they are cut from a different cloth than the mere commoners around them. They come to expect special treatment, fully believing that they are entitled to it. They come to think of themselves as the business, rather than as part of the team that makes the business possible. This kind of ego inflation can be an early symptom of a fatal disease. Contrast it to the way that Falla credits the success of the lingerie that her department at Playtex produces: "*Ours*. It's not mine, or yours. It's *ours*. Because, at the end of the day, it's everybody's contribution that brings the products together. It's not just you—or me. Because I don't contribute all by myself. Even if I came up with this product concept all by myself, and didn't have a support staff, it wouldn't go anywhere. It would have remained an idea. Because we need each other to make it happen."

Dame Anita Roddick

When Anita Roddick founded The Body Shop, she had no idea that in a few short years the company would be opening outlets in shopping malls all over the world. Although there have been ups and downs along the way, including some recent reversals in some of the company's attempts to expand, its rapid success in a market dominated by giant cosmetics firms has been nothing short of phenomenal. Much of this success can be attributed to Roddick's radically new approach to beauty and body care. This fresh approach resonated immediately with women looking for a more wholesome and "natural" way to care for their physical appearance. In an industry that packages new concepts on a daily basis—and then markets them with exorbitantly financed campaigns—how did Roddick's ideas stand out from the rest? And where did she get the ideas that built her company and changed an entire industry to boot?

In Roddick's case, the inspiration came from what she calls a humanitarianism that has guided all the important choices in her adult life. Put simply, her humanitarian impulses have determined the kinds of relationships she has had with people who have been crucial to The Body Shop's success. First and foremost among these people were women in developing countries whose native methods of bodily care became Roddick's signature product. Roddick's admiration for these women, and her fascination with their culture, enabled her to learn from what they were doing and establish highly generative business relationships with them. Listening to, learning from, and conducting successful business with indigent tribal women from many parts of the world requires a number of capacities that spring directly from a humanitarian orientation: deep inter-

Dame Anita Roddick

est in people from all backgrounds, respect for people with different knowledge and skills than yourself, humility with respect to the wisdom of people without formal education, and trust in their capacities to deal honestly and responsibly with an outsider.

Roddick began her journey into the minds and practices of these women quite literally with a journey—a series of travels to the Third World that she did when in her twenties. Even at the time she had a sense that these were more than recreational trips. Roddick sees journeying as a way of playing out the sense of human connection—the humanitarianism—that guides her life. The journeys offered her a broad mix of intellectual, personal, and moral benefits, including observations, ideas, contacts, self-reflection, and opportunities for service. "So the things I put into my life are journeys, and I think journeys create insights. . . . My job is, how do you [create] a value system where humanity, community is part of the system? So I journey. I do remarkable journeys. I think that I could name a hundred and one things. I could name the prisoners of conscience we got released. The people's lives that you save."

The reciprocal interplay of learning from and teaching, inspiring and becoming inspired by, profiting from and contributing to characterizes the humanitarian orientation that guides Roddick's working relations. It is not merely that Roddick conducts her affairs this way out of a sense of duty. She finds the very roots of her success in her attitude of respect and concern for the women she meets on her travels. As she told me:

The travels that I did for years in the sixties, traveling around the world, living in these preindustrial communities, gives you an edge. And it doesn't take long to realize that you can wash your hair with almost anything. You don't carry a shampoo bottle with you when you're stuck in some village in South Africa or somewhere.

I think my success comes through the ability to gather around women and get their stories out of them and the stories of the rituals of the body. I think I've done that. So when I opened the shop, I had all these amazing stories. Like, "Oh, I was in Sri Lanka and the women would eat the pineapples and not throw the skins away and rub it on their body." And years later you realize it's because this particular protein that gets rid of God-knows-what in there, acid. . . . I'm a storyteller, so people love that. I think that was part of the success.

What began as youthful curiosity and enthusiasm for the practices of native cultures matured into a systematic method of examining these practices and adapting them for universal uses. Roddick speaks of this method almost the way that an anthropologist describes ethnography, as an exercise in storytelling. But in Roddick's case it was storytelling that addressed a pointed business question: how can the health-care practices of these native women teach us lessons that will help The Body Shop stand out in the crowded and poorly served cosmetics market? Roddick was always conscious of what she was after while she was listening to the stories of native women in faraway lands.

To this day she credits these narrative exchanges with the radical concepts that set The Body Shop apart from the rest of its industry. These exchanges provided fuel for Roddick's vital moral imagination: "Part of the success was sticking two fingers up to the cosmetics industry. It's an overpackaged industry. Plays on women's fears. It's bloody boring, if you ask me, because all that says is, 'Shut up, get a face-lift, or diet!' So being able to challenge that, it's really easy, let me tell you. This is not rocket science. It's so bloody easy to go in the opposite direction of the cosmetics industry. It's so easy because they all say the same things, do the same things, use the same language. It's easy to come in like this kid who just says, 'Give me a break!' We were going the route of indigenous people's wisdom."

Roddick's creative gift was the capacity to look at what indigenous people were doing with fresh eyes and learn from their wisdom. Now that she has proven the commercial value of this strategy, many others are following similar paths, but when she founded The Body Shop, Roddick was essentially alone in her approach. It was an approach founded on a deep respect for the native people whom she journeyed across the world to meet, as well as an antipathy for the inadequate ways that women were being served by the cosmetics industry of the time. Her sharp sense of business opportunity coupled with her burning desire to succeed fueled Roddick's moral imagination and gave her the necessary competitive advantage to stand out from the rest of this crowded industry.

John Sperling

The University of Phoenix, John Sperling's brainchild, is the centerpiece of the Apollo Group, a large and rapidly growing corporation that not only has made Sperling and his investors wealthy but that is also transforming the face of higher education. This publicly traded corporation has brought professional education to many thousands of adults who otherwise would not have had the chance to pursue advanced degrees. With campuses all across the Americas and parts of Europe, the University of Phoenix is fast becoming the world's largest provider of academic programs to adults. The university also has become known as a pioneer of "distance learning" through its on-line course offerings. In these and many other ways, Sperling's creation is a trendsetter in a field that often resists change and innovation. And the business is highly profitable, as the rising price of its shares in the midst of a brutal bear market attests.

Because change—and especially market-driven change—does not come easily to the education establishment, Sperling has had to fight many battles to bring his concept to reality. He has been vilified by the higher education community as a crass opportunist, and he is forever waging trench warfare on the political front to get Phoenix its necessary approvals and accreditations. These fights have left Sperling angry yet wholly undeterred. "I hated the bastards," he

John Sperling

told me, referring to the higher education establishment that tried to block his business plans. He has learned to be "utterly indifferent to disapproval": "So I didn't give a goddamn what the professoriat or the establishment thought about me. I thought they were a bunch of idiots anyway. Not idiots, but they were a bunch of people who were unthinkingly defending their own turf without enlarging their vision of what education should be."

Sperling gets especially incensed when he speaks about a time when the higher education lobby succeeded in stopping Apollo from starting a trade-school business. This was his attempt to bring Phoenix-type instruction to the economically disadvantaged, and he was defeated because he could not prevent a sizable number of these students from dropping out. This opened his trade-school business to criticism that it was not meeting Department of Education regulations, a criticism that Sperling feels was exploited at the expense of the many disadvantaged students who had stayed in and were well served by the school: "The higher education establishment demanded the same metrics for these lower orders as you have at a state university. They're immoral, heartless sons of bitches, and I think they know not what they do. They are so absolutely tunnel-visioned, and their desire to help the lower orders is zero, absolutely zero."

Nevertheless, despite all the friction and hard feelings, Sperling is slowly winning over the higher-education establishment. A recent issue of *Dean and Provost,* a newsletter for traditional college administrators, lauded the University of Phoenix for its innovative approach to learning.[4] It noted that the university's approach has much to offer the adult students who constitute its primary market. The article points out that when the university was founded in 1976, it was "revolutionary." Most institutions of higher learning at that time ignored the adult market entirely. "There were few, if any, night classes, accelerated programs, or programs offering credit for learning outside the classroom. No one talked about customer service for any students." The article concludes that one of the "lessons learned" from Sperling's revolutionary approach is that "competition in any form may lead to a re-evaluation of your institution's programs and services. And that's a good thing for students." Such favorable recognition by the very establishment that the University of Phoenix long fought represents a major victory for Sperling and his Apollo group and is a testimony to the value of his creative achievement.

How did Sperling do it? He began with a philosophy of education based on three principles, each with moral overtones: (1) everyone who wants an advanced education deserves a chance to pursue one, (2) people learn best through community, and (3) learning is what makes people human. Sperling has "absolute moral certainty" about these principles, and they form the basis of his creative vision.

The belief that everyone deserves the chance to pursue an advanced degree led Sperling to develop professional programs for working adults. This turned out to be a brilliant marketing strategy as well as a matter of principle: at the time, working adults were an underserved part of the student population, and they could afford to pay for courses that would further their careers. Sperling's idea that people "learn effectively and joyously if they are part of a learning community" led him to develop an innovative peer-group approach to higher education, which is now admired in the field. In the University of Phoenix model, every student becomes a member of a study group, and half of all assignments are done by the group as a whole rather than by the individual student. The concept that learning is what makes people human motivates everything that Sperling does. He told me that promoting this principle is the best way to avoid the Hobbesian nightmare of living lives that are nothing more than "short, nasty, and brutish."

Sperling's morally backed philosophy not only generated this innovative approach, but it also helped him sustain it in the face of withering attacks and, even more problematic from a business perspective, absolute skepticism on the part of the investment community. "I couldn't get anyone to give me a dime," he recalled. "No venture capitalist would give me the time of day." So Sperling started with $26,000 of his own savings. "I knew I felt alone—I *was* alone." But he also remembers never feeling discouraged or intimidated: "I just felt that it was a very steep hill to climb."

On his way up that hill, Sperling encountered unusually vicious headwinds, even when compared with today's competitive business climate. Not only was his company under attack from its competitors (in this case, the nonprofit colleges and universities) but also from their allies in the government and the press. Sperling was personally excoriated every step along the way—for selling out, for cheapening a noble profession, and for doing away with treasured academic practices such as tenure and full-time faculty. Commonly described as a "diploma mill," Sperling's university was roundly condemned for lacking traditional assets such as a big campus with libraries and gyms.

But his approach had little to do with the physical plant. Sperling wanted his courses to be offered in places and at times that best suited his students. He realized that courses taught locally in the evenings would give working adults far greater access than they could have found in most of the college campuses at the time. And he was early in recognizing that excellent library access can be found on-line.

Sperling also was more concerned about the content of courses than about the composition of his faculty. He realized that if he hired working professionals to teach his courses, he would gain the flexibility to offer standardized curricula with learning objectives carefully crafted to his students' needs. Expert consultants could develop courses that a part-time faculty would be glad to teach. In this manner, Sperling placed the student—rather than the faculty member—at the center of his instructional agenda. Although this strategy evoked the wrath of the professoriat, it had obvious appeal to the consumer-savvy, self-starting adults who are Sperling's primary student market.

On the management front, Sperling emphasizes truthfulness and free speech, moral values that he has shown to have great practical importance. He is careful to cultivate these values in all his employees, so that he can then trust them to represent the company with integrity when they attain positions of leadership. "You have to teach them to tell the truth," he says, indicating that this is not as straight a shot as it might sound. "The truth is very, very painful most of the time. And you just say, you can't tell different things to different people." Truth goes hand in hand with free speech, which Sperling has written into his company's core ethical charter: "It's announced every year, reaffirmed every year, and we expect all employees to have a card with the free speech ethic in their cubicle, in their office, so that everyone is constantly made aware of it.": He continues: "We have a free speech policy in all these companies, so that anyone can talk to anyone about anything at any time. And if they can't, we have a mechanism called 'Comments to the Chairman,' and if any employee feels his or her voice is being restricted in any way, they just write me a letter or leave me an e-mail or a voice mail. And you can get fascistic elements out of the company pretty fast."

The management result of all this is an institutionalized sense of honesty and trust that fosters experimentation and open feedback. This atmosphere makes possible the kind of orderly change that has made the university a symbol of bold progress within higher education. Because Sperling takes such pains to cultivate honest exchange among his employees, he looks to them first for promotions within the company—a sign of trust that further enhances employee morale: "We've got something like 110 campuses now across the country, and there's a great sense of security when you send loyal employees out to start a new one. You don't have to worry about it. They know how to do it. They'll do it. In running all these controversial companies for twenty-five years now, no employee has ever gone to the press with horror stories or anything like that. So you have to have absolute integrity within the company so that there's no doubt what the ethics are."

Mike Murray

When I interviewed Mike Murray, he was vice president for human resources and administration at Microsoft, in charge of the vast personnel division at the world's premier software company. Although he was then a youthful man in his forties, his executive position at Microsoft actually was the capstone of a distinguished career in the high-tech industry. His was a career marked by innovation and creative flair: for example, one of his early achievements at Apple Computer was helping to arrange the famous 1984 Super Bowl commercial in which Apple memorably defined its image as a torch-bearing liberator from the gray-flannel mentality of such competitors as IBM. At Microsoft, however, Murray was in a strictly administrative position, overseeing personnel matters that are often thought to be routine and bureaucratic.

The true measure of any person is how he or she responds to situations that discourage his or her best instincts. Murray's orientation to his administrative charge was anything but routine and bureaucratic. In fact, what struck me was his determination to do things in a way that promoted the highest purposes of the company as a whole. Murray's purpose-driven approach required a whole new look at the procedures and incentives of the personnel system that he was managing. It called for the same kinds of creative talents that Murray had shown in his prior entrepreneurial roles, but this time in service of his administrative responsibilities. Murray's case shines as an example of applying the moral imagination to the most mundane management matters.

Murray knew well what he was up against when he took the job. The situational constraints of the position were accompanied by a demoralizing bias that permeated the executive ranks. He told me: "American business has a general suspicion and in some cases disdain of the personnel practice, and I understand that. I used to be on the

Mike Murray

other side of the fence for years as a line manager or a marketing manager or general manager, and I viewed the people in these kinds of organizations as kind of necessary people to make sure benefit plans were put together and pay practices were consistent, but I never viewed it as a strategic function that could impact the company."

As Murray reflected on the company's basic purpose, however, he saw his human resource work in a different light. He infused his managerial role with his sense of Microsoft's purpose:

> In our kind of business, we are one of the pure intellectual asset-plays in the market today, meaning our assets are not some big piece of machinery in a factory, bolted to the factory floor. Our assets are the ideas that come out of the brains of our people. . . . In fact, we are obligated as the employer to provide a compelling environment so they'll want to come here rather than to one of our competitors. We've got to provide them with complete information; information is power, so you want to have a very powerful workforce.
>
> I don't know how you can chain people to the assembly line and say, "Be creative every twenty seconds." In fact, we don't really know how software is created. It comes out of people's minds and it's some science, some engineering discipline, some just wild creativity. So you have this mix and it works for us.

The creativity that Murray sought to foster in his employees is a means to an end that he first envisioned when he began working in the computer industry decades ago. He was taken by the "democratization of technology"—the idea that "by getting technology in the hands of people . . . whether villagers in Bangladesh, or whether they're schoolteachers or whether they're *Fortune* 500 CEOs, good stuff is going to happen. Let's lower the price, make it easy to use, and populate the world with it." In this way, Murray says that he was "incredibly idealistic" and still retains the "idealism of wanting to make this a better place." From the start, he says, "I had the feeling that what I was doing had some real purpose to it."

Murray's sense of purpose drove his concern not only for his companies' products (in this case, computers and software) but also for the way that they were produced (by the employees' hard work and creativity). In fact, Murray sees the two as inextricably intertwined: the best work is done by workers who are treated fairly and respectfully. In this regard, he notes with admiration a comment that Bill Hewlett made shortly before he died. When asked to name the crowning achievement of his life, Hewlett chose the creation of the HP culture, known as the "HP Way"—a set of ethical standards that expressed the company's commitment to treating its employees honorably.

Murray followed in the Hewlett tradition in his efforts to create personnel practices that maximized workers' creative potentials through respectful treatment. He especially abhors the too common business practice of treating employees as nothing more than a means to the company's ends—the idea that "whatever means it took to get to the end is okay, in terms of the way you manipulate people, yell at them, take them apart, destroy them, whatever." The "HP Way" showed Murray that people who build their companies on a sounder set of human relationships not only build great companies but also take great satisfaction from doing so. The implementation of the "HP Way" was "the most important thing I did in my life."

In the deepest sense, Murray's sense of purpose reflects his spiritual faith. He is far from alone among the businesspeople whom we interviewed. As I've discussed in other chapters, a quiet religiosity or spirituality is often a pronounced part of many successful business leaders. But Murray is especially articulate in integrating his business mission with his religious beliefs. He sees his quest for creativity, in both himself and the employees in his charge, as directly benefiting from the inspiration that he receives from his faith in God. The benefits can be direct or indirect but are always linked to a moral and ethical life:

> Prayer is the belief that God can provide inspiration for you in all aspects of your life. Now sometimes you may have to tough it out on your own, because it's a required learning experience. Other times, and this is my own set of experiences but I can't deny them, ideas get planted in your brain that have no business being there, and I can only think that they are coming through God.
>
> And I'm not saying I sit here every day and say, "What should I do next, God?" and He tells me. Not at all—that's silly. They happen occasionally and often times when you're not expecting it, but probably you won't get the privilege of having spiritual inspiration if you are doing rotten things in your life. If you're cheating, if you're lying, if you're stealing, if you're being bad, if you're corrupting your mind with stuff that pollutes it, I don't know how you're going to feel the truth coming into you.

As explored throughout this chapter, the moral imagination plays multiple roles in business, some on the production side and some on the management side. It contributes to the generation of new ideas for products and services; it provides a backbone of support for these ideas when they seem risky or unproven; it suffuses these ideas with a magnetic energy that communicates the value of the ideas throughout the company; and it can help managers create ways to solve personnel problems and establish a workplace environment that maximizes their employees' potential. All these uses of moral imagination are driven by a sense of purpose. The purpose, if it is to be truly inspirational for oneself and others, usually includes service to the customer, service to the company, or, beyond that, service to one's deepest beliefs about the meaning of one's life. In many cases these beliefs emanate from religious or spiritual faith, and even when they are strictly secular in nature, they often still have a transcendent quality. This is reminiscent of the ancient notion of "calling," the idea that one feels called by a higher power to dedicate one's work to a noble purpose.

Time and again, I heard these sentiments expressed by the successful business leaders I interviewed. Their particular purposes were varied, and the work that they did included all the assignments and responsibilities that people in business assume. Yet their sentiments were the same in all cases: work has meaning to the extent that it reflects a true purpose; a business career succeeds to the extent that it has meaning; and finding meaning and success in one's work—any kind of work—is a creative act, relying on moral imagination.

4 Empathic Morality and the Golden Rule

Try a fascinating experiment in moral development with any group of five-year-olds. First, tell them the Golden Rule. Say it in a couple of different ways, both in its traditional form ("Do unto others as you would have them do unto you") and in a plainer English version, making sure that they understand all the words (for example, "Treat other people just the same as you'd like them to treat you"). Then ask the five-year-olds to repeat the Golden Rule and give some examples of the way it works. Unless they are prodigies, most of the children will repeat the Golden Rule as something like, "Do back to other people what they do to you," or "Treat other people in the same way that they treat you." Most five-year-olds will come up with the following kinds of examples: "I gave my Mom a nice birthday present because she's always nice to me," "Billy's my best friend, and I share my bike with him so he'll let me use his bike," or "You can fight with someone who hits you first."

Now as adults, we recognize that such sentiments are closer to the "eye for an eye" ethic of reciprocity and revenge than they are to the Golden Rule ethic of "love thy neighbor as thyself." We recognize this because we are able to do an extra mental step that most five-year-olds cannot do: we consider what we would want if we were the other, instead of what we do want as ourselves. We are not bound by a limited, self-centered perspective that dictates how we feel when someone has done something to us (or for us), or that prescribes how we should act if we want to get someone to do something for us. We can take an extra mental step (a "what we would want if we were the other" step) by mentally placing ourselves in the shoes of another person. As this cognitive transaction is called in developmental psychology, adults can "role-take."[1] In this way, we can know the wishes and expectations of another person.

Most adults are capable of the perspective-taking skills needed to understand the Golden Rule. Indeed, most children by the age of eight or nine can do it. But this does not mean that most adults actually use the Golden Rule in their day-to-day relationships, especially in their business transactions. Some people, first and foremost, are out for themselves: they couldn't care less what another person would want, so the Golden Rule never comes up. And some adults persist in applying the Golden Rule in the manner of a five-year-old—as a justification for bribery or revenge ("I treat them as they treat me"). Still others may apply the Golden Rule to their closest loved ones— their children, their spouses, their friends—but assume that the world beyond their most intimate circles is a Darwinian environment where survival depends on more cutthroat behavior.

The Golden Rule's Empathic Heart and Soul

To use the Golden Rule regularly, we need not only to understand what it means (in an adult way rather than a child's tit-for-tat manner) but also to care enough about other people to treat them well. This feeling of *caring* about others is usually called *empathy,* and it is one of the hottest topics in social-science research these days, in part because of its importance in positive human relationships and in part because of recent breakthroughs in the study of the brain, showing that empathy is hardwired in humans from birth.[2] If perspective-taking is the "mind" of the Golden Rule, empathy is its heart and soul. When the capacities for perspective-taking and empathy are cultivated, resources of great personal and social power are acquired.

Empathy is the emotional capacity to experience another person's pleasure or pain. It provides the emotional urge to care about other people. The expressions "My heart bleeds for you," or "He's a bleeding heart" (when meant seriously rather than sarcastically) are intended to capture the empathic sharing of emotion that leads to acts of charity and other benevolent behavior. Without empathy, the world would be a far more harsh and unforgiving place. It is one of the primary "moral emotions" with which the species has been endowed as part of its adaptive genetic legacy.[3] Because empathy is such a central part of the "kinder and gentler" dimension of human life, it is easy to overlook its practical and instrumental importance. Yet empathy, like all moral emotions, enhances ones own interests while it serves those of others. It does so in ways direct and indirect, immediate and long-term. The better a person becomes at using empathy, the greater the benefits all around.

The capacity to experience another person's pleasure or pain through empathy is part of our native endowment as humans. Every human being is born with the capacity to empathize with others. Newborns cry when they hear crying sounds, and they show signs of pleasure at such happy sounds as cooing and laughter. By the second year of life, it is common for children to comfort peers or parents in distress. But our capacity for empathy does not remain fixed at birth; rather, it must improve with learning if it is to become an effective part of our responses to social situations. For example, the comfort that young children offer loved ones is not always appropriate to the person they are trying to help. Psychologists have pointed to such examples as toddlers offering mothers their own security blankets when they perceive that their moms are upset.

Although the emotional disposition to help is present at the beginning of life, the means of helping others effectively must be learned and refined through social experience. Moreover, in many people, the capacity for empathy may fail to grow—and it can even diminish—over time. People can act horribly cruelly to those with whom they refuse to empathize. For example, a New York City policeman who asked a teenage thug how he could have crippled an eighty-three-year-old woman during a mugging got the reply: "Why should that bother me? She's not me."[4]

Developing your capacity for empathy means mentally putting yourself in the shoes of as many types of people as you can—people who look different than you do, who think differently, who come from different backgrounds or are in different social positions or are living in different circumstances. It is not always easy to do this. You need to take a mental leap into another's world and come away understanding not only how that person is different from you but also how your fates are entwined. You must care about the other in an emotional sense while perceiving the other accurately in an intellectual sense. This capacity is the psychological foundation of the Golden Rule. As a product of moral imagination that is driven by empathy, the Golden Rule is a different sort of creative act than those discussed in Chapter 3. It is a creative act that is particularly helpful in dealing with clients, customers, employees, or partners.

The CEO who starts in the company's mailroom may gain insights into the needs and desires of entry-level employees, but it is easy enough for the CEO to forget or ignore such insights after climbing the corporate ladder. Similarly, all businesspeople are consumers of things, but that does not mean that they always keep their consumers' best interests in mind while marketing goods to them.

To genuinely take into account the interests of another, you first must understand the perspective of the person who is in a different situation; then you must choose to empathize with that person. This act of moral imagination has both a cognitive component (perspective-taking) and an emotional one (empathy). Together, the two capacities create a strong sense of identification with the other people who populate your working world—a sense of identification that is essential for such key transactions as collaborating with fellow workers, serving customers, managing employees, and communicating with investors.

This chapter is about businesspeople who regularly use perspective-taking, empathy, and the Golden Rule in their day-to-day transactions. They have found these capacities to be formulas for successful and satisfying business relations, even in the midst of temptations and pressures to treat someone shabbily. How do they actually do this? What can we learn from their experience?

Leon Gorman

Using Empathy and the Golden Rule Successfully

About a quarter of the business leaders whom we interviewed said spontaneously that they relied on the Golden Rule to guide their working relations. It is striking that such a sizable proportion of businesspeople mentioned the same notion without thinking twice. The principle was clearly at the forefront of their thinking, since they invoked it without specific prompting. Other interviewees spoke about their interpersonal relations in a manner highly consistent with the Golden Rule, and they likely would have been quick to acknowledge its validity if asked.

For example, Leon Gorman, the CEO of the legendary Maine department store L. L. Bean, said, "We're committed to the Golden Rule, and we try to make decisions from what looks like it will be best for the overall value of our stakeholders." By *stakeholders,* Gorman meant everyone in the company's broad universe, including shareholders, employees, customers, and members of the local community. In a similar vein, Mike Markkula, a co-founder of Apple Computer and Echelon Corporation, said that, of all the beliefs that played a role in his success, "the Golden Rule is the one that I would use most commonly." His reflections reveal the empathic concerns that are at the emotional heart of the principle: "I would never ask someone to do a job that I wouldn't do myself. I never put someone in a position that I wouldn't want to be in. That

Mike Markkula

has always been part of my way of interacting with people, whether it's the janitor or the vice president of engineering, or whatever."

But for Markkula, as for others we interviewed, the Golden Rule is not simply a feel-good way of expressing empathy and kindness toward a fellow human being. Rather, it has crucial practical value in promoting the trust that is needed for any business deal. Markkula explained: "Trust is invaluable. You can get all the lawyers you want around this table, and you and I can write a contract about something and cover all the 'what ifs' and the 'so forths' and the 'so ons.' Say I am going to manufacture something for you, and we get it all down, and I do the best I can and something isn't right. Well, if you and I trust one another we can talk about that, we can work it out. We can change the contract if it turns out no longer to be a fair deal. . . . If you don't observe the Golden Rule, I don't think you'll be able to develop that kind of trust."

Another information technology executive, Mike Hackworth, the CEO of Cirrus Technology in the 1990s and a board member at several other large corporations, also attributed much of his success to the Golden Rule. Hackworth is aware that the Golden Rule requires a combination of empathy and perspective-taking skill; in fact, he pretty much used those terms when speaking of his debt of gratitude to this very principle. When asked which of his personal qualities was most crucial to his achievements, Hackworth remarked: "One that comes to mind here, interestingly, is empathy. I think that one of the

Mike Hackworth

things that has helped me tremendously in my career is that I could put myself in the other guy's shoes."

Hackworth's introspections on his own use of perspective-taking and empathy show how these acts of moral imagination yield unique advantages in the business world, much like the creative uses of the moral imagination that I discussed in Chapter 3. In his inventive approach to salesmanship, Hackworth demonstrates the value of his empathic capacities in a marketing context: "An early part of my career was in selling and marketing, and the important thing that helped me there was . . . I had this different model where you're trying to reflect the needs of the customer and the capabilities of the supplier and match those up. To the extent that you could match them up, you'd be a successful sales[person]. To the extent that there wasn't a match, you either go find another customer or go find another company to work for, because you don't have a basis for a matched transaction. So anyway, getting into all that, my empathy was very key, because I could sit down with the customers and understand their needs. So I think empathy had a lot to do with that."

Empathy helps businesspeople accomplish goals that otherwise might be beyond their reach. Hackworth noted the importance of empathy for communicating with customers in a marketing relationship. His point is that finding the right match between what one has to offer and what the customer needs is critical to any business transaction, and too often a deal will fall through because one of the parties sees this as an all-or-nothing matter, thinking, "We're either

Dyana King

a good match or we're not." Yet in many cases, there is a potential for creating an alignment between supplier and customer. A deep understanding built on empathy is the surest route to this end.

Empathic understanding also enables managers to work productively with their employees. Dyana King, one of the principals at Thinknicity, a high-tech recruitment firm, said that her goal at the company is to "create an environment and a culture where people want to work, where people want to come to be part of a 'destination company' . . . just because it's the greatest place to be." To accomplish that, King says that she "pays attention" to the special characteristics of each person working for her. She deals with employees as individuals, taking care to understand their particular needs and circumstances.

"Every person is different," she said, "and you have to deal with them on their own terms." This requires practicing some intricate mental manipulations, such as reconstructing her own perspective to recall an earlier point in her career: "I try to put myself in the shoes of where I was when I was learning this. What were the things that I learned, the little lights that came on for me. Those little 'aha!' moments. And I try to think about those and relate it back to the people that I've hired, and everybody's different. A lot of people learn the way I do, and some people don't learn the way I do, which is more of a challenge. I have to think of a different way of presenting them with the information that's going to be meaningful to them."

King uses her empathy skills to cultivate clients in a hotly competitive industry, and to work with them (in her phrase, to "educate them") so that she can provide valuable services that set her apart from her competitors. "We're not just a body shop. We actually seek to add value to your [a client's] hiring process through partnering with you and understanding what your needs are and delivering what you need instead of fifty résumés that I just pulled off the Internet."

King's commitment to empathic understanding gives her both a practical advantage as well as an enduring sense of personal satisfaction in her career. On the practical front, she notes that a lot of the competitors who tried to make it in a quick and sleazy way (the "dirty dogs," she calls them) are no longer on the scene in the wake of the dot-com crash. "The Crash!" she exclaims. "But you know what? We're still here." On the personal front, she gives testament to the deepest significance of the moral advantage: "I can sleep at night. That's more important to me. Like I said, there are a lot of people in our business [who] are strictly motivated by money, and for me personally it's more than that. I figure that if you run a business above board, you treat your clients with respect and dignity, with honesty and integrity, they will come back to you again and again, and there you'll have the money part. . . . [But] we're a company that's about more than making money."

Using the Golden Rule to Solve
Difficult Management Problems

Beyond its usefulness for cultivating positive and advantageous business relationships, the Golden Rule serves as an effective problem-solving tool when those relationships threaten to turn sour. Business always has a defensive and tough-minded side, even when carried out in the most purposeful manner. Success in business calls for hard decisions that can create conflict with employees and other stakeholders. These decisions can be made in a high-handed manner with macho flair ("It's my way or the highway"); or they can be made with responsiveness to the needs of those affected by the decisions.

I have found that successful business leaders eschew the macho swagger of the callous and insensitive route. They make tough decisions when they need to, but they do so in a respectful manner, minimizing the damage rather than gratuitously adding insult to injury. In the words of the CEO of a major oil company: "I also believe, on the other side of the spectrum, that you must—and this is something that I've had to learn in my career—you must treat people with respect. I know it's basic, but if you're going to be tough, you better treat people with respect. You better treat people exactly the same way you expect to be treated."

Over and over again, we heard the phrase "dignity and respect" from the business leaders who have made their mark in managing employees effectively. The attitude permeates their daily interactions with their subordinates, and it springs directly from the understandings and feelings underlying the Golden Rule. Often the interviewees uttered that phrase and the Golden Rule in the same breath, as in the case of Dickie Sykes, the equal employment officer at AMEC Construction Management: "I make sure that, number one, I treat everyone with dignity and respect. That I try, even with my own staff, not to speak with them when I'm really angry, because it clouds up your judgment. So I try to calm down first and try to take a more realistic approach to why someone did what they did, and to always start off with praise before criticizing. So those are the things that I try to bring to my day-to-day work environment. And I think that most people want to come to work and be treated with dignity and respect, and be treated fairly. So if I want to be treated that way, why wouldn't everyone else?"

In business, the classic issue that sets management in opposition to labor is unionization. In many cases, a drive to unionize has national rather than local origins: an organization such as the AFL-CIO launches an initiative to increase membership, and as part of that initiative, employees at a local shop are vigorously recruited. Whether or not the local labor situation before the union drive was problematic—and even in the best of circumstances, some employees will always have certain grievances—the very possibility of unionizing inevitably raises tensions between labor and management. A manager's response to these tensions will determine the quality and effectiveness of a company's working environment for years to come.

Rebecca Kaufman

One response is to go along with the drive to unionize, and in many cases this may be the only realistic option. But some companies—in particular, smaller or newer companies with shaky capitalization—cannot afford to pay union wages and remain competitive. From their perspective, capitulating to union demands would mean losing their business and letting their employees go, which seems like something of a Hobson's choice as far as employee relations are concerned. So, many businesses stonewall all union demands, refusing to consider any and all related issues, out of fear of ending up on the wrong side of organizing drives and labor laws.

For managers who believe that unionization threatens their company's survival, there are ways to respond that still preserve positive and productive employee relations. The key to these ways is the empathic understanding at the heart of the Golden Rule. For example, Susan Davis, the president (and co-founder with Rebecca Kaufman) of a small Seattle-based costume company called Period Corsets, described her strategy with respect to a possible union drive in this way:

> And as far as we know, nobody asked our employees to join the union or not, but the union asked to meet with us, and we tried to understand from them what the benefits would be to having our shop be union, and as far as we could tell, they didn't give us any because our employees were satisfied. They probably would have made more money, but we would have gone out of business. . . . I've always thought that if I were still working in the

Susan Davis

opera workroom when they voted in the union, I don't know if I would have voted for the union, but if the union had been voted in while I was in the workroom, I would have been extremely involved in the union, very proactive, very interested in making sure that it was doing the best it could for everyone there. So . . . it's not that I don't support the union, because I think that in that position I would have, but it didn't have any benefits for our shop.

Here Davis mentally puts herself in the shoes of workers who might find a union appealing by imagining what her own reactions to unionization might have been when she was employed in the workroom. In this way, she determines with some confidence that she can address her employees' needs without jeopardizing the business. She considers that, first, they are better off with a job in a nonunion shop than without a job in a union shop. Second, she figures that "the more products we sell, the more we will be able to pay them, because our cost of goods won't go up tremendously." With good employee relations, Davis expects increased productivity and profits, some of which she can pass on to workers in the form of improved pay and benefits. Third, even now, Davis looks for ways to do "little bits" here and there that signal goodwill to employees without bankrupting the company: paid leaves and holidays, subsidized lunches, and so on. Most important is an atmosphere of trust that she communicates with small but significant gestures:

One of our employees . . . has worked in lots of different places, and worked for the Post Office, and utilities companies, and other jobs, and he's worked for us for two-and-a-half years and he's astounded by things that will still come up. He'll ask us about something, an appointment he forgot to tell us about and he's going to be gone for an hour and hopes that's okay. Our reply is: John, if it's a doctor's appointment, you write sick time on your timesheet. If it's not, it's up to you. Make up the hour if you need the money, don't if you don't. He's still startled that we respect that he has a life outside of work and that he has other obligations that don't involve us. And it's always gratifying to know that it brings some ease to his life that he doesn't have to accommodate us all the time—and we also do the same for him.

The constant role-reversal that Davis uses in thinking about how to treat employees gives her a palpable sense of satisfaction when she feels that she has done something to improve their situation; and she expects that they will feel the same about the company and those who run it. This attitude is almost a working definition of shared empathy. It should be clear how a mutual empathic understanding of this kind is in the best interests of everyone working at the company. It brings home, in a way that is backed up by the full force of emotion, the salutary ethic that everyone is "in it together." The fates of the leaders and the employees are intermingled: that is, "Your success rides on my success, and vice versa." What better way could there be to harness everyone's energies to a common cause?

Naturally, this approach leads to more productive employee relations than the "us-against-them" stance that usually predominates when labor concerns arise. The key is the more inclusive approach that comes from concerted perspective-taking efforts. Perspective-taking transforms a self-centered orientation ("What is this company doing for me?") into a mutual point of view ("How can we best succeed together?"), turning a potential source of negativism into positive streams of energy. In this way, it becomes possible for every worker to identify with the company's overall mission and to find personal meaning in the company's work. In the long run, this creates the kind of morale that inspires trust, loyalty, and an attitude of heartfelt service among employees—an atmosphere that could not be bought by salaries and perks alone, no matter how extravagant they may be.

The Golden Rule mandate of imagining yourself in the position of the other, if followed consistently, promotes solidarity among people who work together, because it gives them a real basis for mutual trust. In business, this applies to employers and employees, vendors and clients, merchants and customers, entrepreneurs and investors, companies and communities, and so on: virtually any human relationship can be ameliorated through the Golden Rule. The only problem is that it can be difficult to imagine yourself in the position of others who seem radically different than you. This is where a commitment to perspective-taking comes in: the process of placing yourself in another's shoes requires a concerted effort to cultivate a moral imagination that paves the way for empathy and the Golden Rule. It is an effort that is well-rewarded, benefiting the self as well as the other by establishing the foundations of productive working relations.

Using the Golden Rule to Clarify the Mission of One's Business

Positive human relations in business is a primary benefit of employing the Golden Rule, but it is not the only one. For some, the Golden Rule clarifies the very mission of their work. Especially in times of hesitation and doubt, this can provide a sense of direction and a will to persevere. It is yet another source of the driving purpose that all successful ventures must draw on from time to time. In this sense, the Golden Rule can operate in much the same way as the purposes discussed in Chapter 3, resulting from a similar use of the moral imagination.

Julie Pearl is the CEO and managing attorney for the Pearl Law Group. Her firm specializes in immigration law, and she said that its "vision" is to become "the business immigration firm of choice." Her decision to focus the firm in this way has contributed greatly to

Julie Pearl

its success at a time of low demand in an overcrowded legal market. But it was not an easy decision. When Pearl was in law school, she told herself, "I'm a generalist." Specializing in immigration work "meant that I had to turn away clients early on, because someone would call and say, 'Hey, I married an Italian, can you help me?' And I would say, 'Nope, sorry.'" But Pearl's sharp focus paid off: her firm now generates enough business to fully employ thirty-plus people, and it is still in a growth mode.

When Pearl talks about legal cases, it is clear that the focus that has so successfully defined her firm's mission emanates from a moral purpose reflecting the Golden Rule. In fact, she has directly embraced the Golden Rule to generate "creative solutions" to intransigent problems that frequently arise in her line of work. For Pearl, the Golden Rule is not only a motivating source of purpose, it is also a source of the moral imagination necessary to win her cases:

> You'll see in our subdefinition [our focus], how we differ in that we explore all lawful immigration options for our clients, and not just the standard approaches, especially in situations that require creative solutions. And that's important, because in our field, it's so easy, for example, if you just say, "Gosh, I just got a call from a guy who is a huge co-founder of a company here, and his immigration department that we don't represent had told him that he should go a standard way of getting a green card, which is really

complicated for him. . . . And he qualifies for a different way (harder for *us* to do), but a lot of other attorneys just don't think about other options because the paralegals are all trained to do the standard way, and we get paid pretty much the same fee regardless of whether we do the hard way or not. With the hard way, we have to prove how special he really is—we have to do a lot of creative writing. But I have always said, "If he were my brother and he needed a green card, what would I do for him?"

For Pearl, taking the role of the other (or, more precisely, the role of the other's sister) triggers an empathic feeling that motivates—in a supercharged manner—her pursuit of creative solutions to knotty immigration problems. In addition, it provides her with an idea of which services her clients will find most useful to help them make informed judgments about their own situations. Along the same lines, Pearl also asks, "How would I give him (my brother) all the knowledge that we have to help him make an informed decision?" Imagining your client as your brother is not the same as imagining your client as yourself, but for Julie Pearl it accomplishes the same empathic purpose, setting the stage for the energetic and creative approach that sets her firm apart from most of her competitors.

Like all the other uses of moral imagination discussed in this book, empathic perspective-taking generates a world of new possibilities that would be impossible to glean from one's own limited worldview. Using empathy, a leader becomes attuned to the needs of others, thereby opening up new possibilities for business success. There is no better way to gain the customer's confidence than by making a concerted effort to thoroughly understand his or her wants and needs.

The Golden Rule as a Way of Life

For some, the Golden Rule ethic of empathy and respect for the other goes far beyond its utility as a winning business strategy. It defines all their business relations, because they consider it a law of life. For example, the CEO of a large restaurant chain said that he is best able to resolve conflicts by taking a sympathetic view of other people's positions, even when he disagrees with them. To accomplish this, he begins by assuming that other people generally operate in good faith. He knows full well that this may not be true of everyone: "There are people who would do anything for a dollar out there, who would step on others without any conscience about it." But this CEO's good-faith assumption applies well enough to most of the people he deals with: "I know the public perception is the opposite—greedy, mean-spirited people [who] don't give a damn—but my experience tells me the opposite: most people are good people."

With this notion as his operating assumption, this CEO is able to get inside the source of potential business conflicts and gain the insight he needs to prevent or resolve said conflicts: "If you assume, when you're listening to them and dealing with them, their best motives as opposed to anything else, at least you'll understand where they are coming from with more clarity. . . . It gives you just a better appreciation of what the other side is saying to you. It doesn't mean that it's right or that it's consistent with your values. But it does give you a better appreciation of where they're coming from and maybe an insight on how to resolve the conflict and deal with the particular business issue. I don't consider it a business strategy. It's a tactic of life."

Such a fundamental law (or "tactic") of life can be discovered through personal experience, or it can be found in spiritual or religious tradition. The Golden Rule has religious roots, and many business leaders consider it to be a mandate of God. For example, Rich DeVos, the chairman and CEO of Amway, explained his allegiance to the Golden Rule in this way: "We start with the premise that we're each created by God and, therefore, we respect each other. So that's just a basic part of my life that you try to live an honest, trustworthy life. Well, that automatically translates into how you deal with your employees. It translates into how you discipline your employees, if you have to. That you don't hit them over the head and throw them out the door because they made a mistake. You have means whereby you sit with them and try to help them get straightened out and get on the right road and get on with it. All those things are part of the general way in which you deal with your business."

What DeVos refers to as a "general way" of doing business is really a total commitment to acting in a manner consistent with the Golden Rule. More than a strategic choice, it is a way of being that follows from a galvanizing vision of the kind of life one wants to live and the kind of person one wants to be. In DeVos's case, the vision is religiously inspired, yet he also is acutely aware of the practical, real-world benefits of his commitment. When everyone in a company is out for themselves, the company inevitably stalls, and everyone pays a price for the self-centered atmosphere. When the Golden Rule ethic is widely shared, however, as DeVos pointed out, the company is in a position to thrive: "There's a wonderful sense of duty and responsibility on the part of most people. Otherwise, the whole system fails. You can't do it by having a policeman at the door or having a truant officer check up on every employee to make sure they are really sick. You work on a matter of trust. That's how the world runs. And when you don't have that trust, the world falls apart. But our world's running pretty good, and that's the world I live in."

The Golden Rule can be many things. It can be an understanding, a feeling, a way of life. I began this chapter by noting the importance of the understanding that the Golden Rule encapsulates: the insight into another's wants and needs that only can be gained by the cognitive process of perspective-taking. I then noted the importance of empathy, a feeling that comes out of the process of sharing emotions with another. Perspective-taking and empathy are essential parts of the Golden Rule and the ethic of mutual respect that it represents. But even these key processes are not the whole story. There is also a philosophical part that can go broader and deeper than the acts of sharing other people's perspectives and emotions.

When a person adopts the Golden Rule because it is an idea that the person truly believes in, it becomes part of the person's moral identity and, eventually, a way of life for that person. It transforms all of the person's relationships, including those with partners, employees, customers, clients, colleagues, and even competitors. This kind of total commitment is not at all incompatible with a strategic use of the Golden Rule simply because it is good policy; in fact, the former may grow out of the latter. But it does create a more reliable tendency to behave according to the rule in all of one's business transactions. It is this consistency that yields the strongest trust, because one acquires a reputation as someone who can be counted on for decency and respectful treatment.

Strategic choices guided by a sure sense of one's best interests are well and good—and in this chapter, as in the rest of the book, I have made the case that the moral way is always in one's long-term best interests. The Golden Rule, along with the perspective-taking and empathy that play it out in everyday transactions, is the moral way when it comes to dealing with other people in business or in other realms of life. Strategic uses of the Golden Rule are constructive and beneficial to all parties. Yet even more powerful and mutually rewarding is a commitment to a belief system and a way of life that encompasses the Golden Rule.

Moral imagination, as I have written, is necessary for the act of transporting yourself into another's thoughts and feelings, just as it is necessary for the creative business insights discussed in Chapter 3. What triggers moral imagination? There are many answers , but one of the most prominent has to do with beliefs that are inspiring and uplifting. In the same way that noble purposes spur the kinds of imaginative moral creativity I wrote about earlier, a belief in the Golden Rule as a purpose in itself leads to a general use of moral imagination for perspective-taking, empathy, and human-relations solutions that are based on mutual respect. A purpose acts as a motivator, fueling the drive to employ your moral imagination, as well as an integrator, keeping you committed to moral imagination in all your transactions.

Every particular decision to do the right thing is a step toward a moral advantage. When unified by an overarching moral purpose, all the separate steps synchronize and pull together with harmony, consistency, and vigor. The particular decisions become dependable and compelling, a cherished part of who you are. As I will explore in the next chapter, this principle also applies to that befuddled aspect of conduct that long has been seen as the most problematic of all: business ethics.

5 | Business Ethics That Come Naturally

> Business ethics means a great deal more
> than obeying the civil law and not obeying
> the moral law. It means imagining and
> creating a new sort of world based on
> the principles of individual creativity,
> community, realism, and other virtues
> of enterprise.
>
> MICHAEL NOVAK, *Business as a Calling*[1]

Across the landscape of business education, from business schools to management training programs, essentially all moral concerns are handled under the rubric of "business ethics." That phrase usually refers to the accepted codes and practices that we need to follow if we wish to stay out of trouble. I do not deny the importance of these codes and practices—they generally have a moral basis, they protect other people's rights, and it behooves everyone to stay out of trouble—but I believe that the narrow and negative way that these "business ethics" are presented in the standard approach does a disservice to the real purposes of ethical commitments. What's more, the way that ethics has been taught in many leading business education programs has done little to ensure actual moral conduct among the students who have taken the program. In fact, there is evidence that this standard approach may even decrease the chance that students will practice moral conduct in day-to-day business settings.[2]

The sociologist Amitai Etzioni has written that, in light of the corporate scandals of the early 2000s, "business schools—the training grounds for corporate tycoons—have been forced to face the fact that they have failed to produce honest brokers."[3] Etzioni observed that business educators feel uncomfortable discussing fundamental moral issues in their classrooms. They wonder whether they may be putting their students at a disadvantage by urging them to adopt ethical restrictions on their competitive drives. When the Harvard Business School introduced a mandatory ethics requirement in the late 1980s, "reactions ranged from disgust to outright hostility." Etzioni noted the following scene in a faculty meeting:

> A member of the marketing department mused that if the latter policy [discussing ethics in all classes] were adopted, his department would have to close because much of what it was teaching constituted a form of dissembling: selling small items in large boxes, putting hot colors on packages because they encourage people to buy impulsively, and so forth.
>
> A finance teacher was also concerned about its effects on his teaching. Students later told me that they learned in his course how you could make a profit by breaking implicit contracts.[4]

To paraphrase an old saw, with teachers like these, the subject of business ethics needs no enemies. It is no wonder that research has found that the typical ethics course has a deleterious impact on students' business behavior. The problem is twofold: first, these programs begin with the cynical assumption that cheating and lying are tempting because they really do help people get ahead in business; and second, the programs compartmentalize ethics into a list of cautionary do's and don'ts that have nothing to do with the aspirations that most strongly drive businesspeople.

With such a mind-set, this approach to business ethics is at best begrudging—or worse, either intentionally or unintentionally sabotaging. Some business educators who feel forced to teach ethics go through the motions without fully believing in what they are doing. The students, of course, notice this disdain and pick up the message that ethics is a matter for show only, to be brushed off as soon as you can get away with it. The whole exercise can become an unstated conspiracy between faculty and students to get through their ethics requirements without too much boat-rocking, ultimately sinking into a sea of self-deception.

For example, the catalog description of an Ethics of Corporate Management course at the University of Michigan says: "The module is not concerned with the personal moral issues of honesty and truthfulness; it is assumed that the students at this university have already formed their own standards on these issues."[5] Yet there is no student body in the world that does not still wrestle with issues of honesty, in their own academic work as well as in their anticipation of the work that the unknown future has in store for them. If business ethics courses choose to avoid this most basic of moral problems, one wonders how these students will get any guidance at all in how to approach their careers with a clear ethical compass.

The often narrow and negative approach to ethics that is prevalent in business-school programs can carry over into the corporate world. For one thing, students bring with them to their jobs the cynical orientation that they have learned at school. Corporations sponsor ethical training programs that are taught in the same manner that shaped students' attitudes back in business school. Thus many businesspeople receive a "re-inoculation" of the maladaptive worldview that distorted their orientation to ethics in the first place.

This maladaptive worldview contrasts sharply with the tack that I have taken in this book, because it takes people in directions that end up being self-defeating and harmful to the public interest (including the interests of the corporation). Throughout this book, in a variety of ways, I make the case that a moral perspective provides a decisive advantage rather than a handicap in business. I do *not* claim that this makes it impossible to fail if you are moral, or the obverse, that those who succeed materially are always moral: of course, it *is* possible to get rich through disreputable actions— people do it all the time. But in the long run, over the course of an entire career, commitment to a moral purpose and to honorable conduct will yield many rewards—materially, personally, and spiritually.

Strong morality, including honorable conduct, is immensely

practical. It enables the moral imagination, a fertile source of creativity; it gives people the staying power to explore a risky avenue of promise; it makes it possible to build the trusting human relations needed for productive business transactions; and, as I show in this chapter, it helps people adopt the ethical course of conduct required for any enduring career without feeling constantly tempted to veer into murkier waters. Unfortunately, it is this view of morality as a valuable, practical instrument of success that has too often been missing from standard approaches to business ethics.[6]

The mistake that too many well-intentioned people in business make is thinking of ethics as an external demand, an unwelcome code that they must abide by for the sake of prudence. This reduces ethics to a set of bloodless restrictions. Naturally anyone with this view will always be seeking ways to get around such restrictions. The philosopher and theologian Michael Novak has pointed out that this paralyzing view of ethics has its roots in the Kantian tradition of defining morality as a duty, a string of "thou shalts" and "thou shalt nots."[7] In contrast, writes Novak, the older Aristotelian tradition viewed ethics as an act of goodness, similar in some ways to a fine athletic performance. Aristotle's metaphor for a good act was an archer hitting his mark. This far more positive perspective sets ethics in the context of the person's natural desires to act in accord with an inspiring ideal. As a rule, people *want* to act right, just as people want to hit their marks in sports, in work, or in any other arena of life. And, as in any other facet of life, ethical "success" requires focus, perseverance, discipline, and commitment.

How do you develop such a commitment? To acquire an abiding commitment to ethical behavior, you must come to understand ethics as part of your total life mission. You cannot compartmentalize: the old "Church on Sunday, work on Monday" chestnut will not do. You must connect the demands of ethics with two things: the purpose that you are trying to accomplish in your work, and the kind of person that you wish to be. When you make that connection in your mind and in your heart, you will treasure, rather than resist, ethical demands, because you will understand that they are means to the ends that you most desire. Most prominent among these ends is becoming as much like your ideal self as you possibly can.

Drawing a connection between ethical behavior and the ideal self is yet another act of moral imagination. Novak writes: "To reflect on ethics, in Aristotle's view, is to try to imagine what sort of person one wishes to be by the end of one's life."[8] Observing people whom you admire for character and integrity can facilitate this reflective process of self-definition. In this way, ethics becomes a key part of your dynamic quest to accomplish your most basic personal aspirations. This is a compelling, flesh-and-blood way to think about ethics, infinitely more motivating than the duty-bound notion of prudential prescriptions.

The Practical Value of Ethics in Business

In our interviews with business leaders, the most telling phrase that we heard with regard to ethical demands was from Akosua Barthwell Evans, the managing and national director of the Diversi-fied Client Group at J. P. Morgan Private Bank: "I am happy to work for a firm that has a commitment to integrity." But why should this commitment make her happy? Evans said, "From the way I was brought up, and watching my parents, one of the things that you have to always maintain is your integrity. Your honesty, your word, and relating to people—these are values that I got from my dad, who was a businessman."

For Evans, words such as *integrity* and *honesty* do not represent disembodied values that lurk somewhere in your conscience, isolated from—or worse, antagonistic to—your real everyday motives. To the contrary, these concepts are as real and as motivating as all your other life goals; and when pursued regularly, they are perfectly consistent with those other goals. Being ethical does more than protect you from disaster. As Evans and several other interviewees noted, it also produces the positive effect of happiness, because it helps you become the kind of person that you ideally imagine yourself to be.

Evans identified her father as the role model who helped her define what kind of a person that was—honest, caring, and so on. Many of the people in our study also cited a parent—most often a mother, but sometimes a father—as an inspirational role model. But this was not universal. Some of the moral mentors cited by our

Akosua Barthwell Evans

business leaders were teachers, employers, military commanders, sports coaches, religious figures, and so on. What they all had in common was that they had exemplified noble virtues in a way that enabled the business leader to see the connection between ethical behavior and the ideal self that he or she wanted to become.

The business leaders interviewed also were acutely aware of the practical value of ethics, not just as a means to the end of personal fulfillment (certainly a most significant end in itself) but also as a means to achieving their business goals. There are two points here that almost all agreed on. First, any gains made by unethical behavior are risky and short-term at best. As the CEO of a multinational natural resources company remarked, "So, do I think you have to be ethical, moral, responsible? You bet! Because if you're not, you're going to get run out on a rail." No one wants to do business with someone who can't be counted on, and one's ethical behavior (or the lack thereof) will determine how people judge one's trustworthiness.

Like many businesspeople, Dyana King, a principal at Think-nicity, has observed her share of people who renege on agreements and do other dishonest things. She is realistic about it, as you must be, and she has learned how to watch out for people like that and to avoid working with them whenever possible. She believes that they are doing themselves and the people they deal with a disservice: "It's short-term gains. I don't think they gain long-term respect in the marketplace. I don't think they build a brand for themselves that's good. . . . I'll never work with them again. Never. . . . In our business, the people that are good, that do good work, you want to know them, you want to have a good relationship with them, because you want to provide your clients with the best people. That's how your clients continue to come back to you. Our business is all about relationships."

Every business is "all about relationships." In some cases, the relationships with investors are primary. The stock manipulation scandals of the early 2000s have shown what can happen when the trust of investors is violated by phony accounting and other acts of deceit. In other businesses, the relationships with customers are key. A business may be able to sell one batch of watered-down wine, but as soon as the word gets out—and it will—the rest of the bottles will stay on that company's shelves.

Ethics as a Preemptive Choice

The second point that successful business leaders agree on is that unethical behavior places your other, nonmonetary business goals at risk. As I have noted throughout this book, most people with successful careers aspire to purposes beyond simply making money, important though that is to them. They want to serve customers, develop new ideas and products, create jobs, make a difference in the world. The CEO of a multinational food service company put it this way: "Money is important for a lot of reasons. It's a psychological reward. It's a scorecard. It's financial security for your family. All these things are important, but it isn't the prime motivator for me." When it comes to an ethical dilemma such as the temptation to increase profits by cutting corners on safety, this CEO's response is unambiguous, indeed practically automatic: "Well, I never would compromise the safety of our customers or employees. Period. Never. All of our people know that. We're just not going to do it. It doesn't matter about profits, it's just one of those things you don't do. It's a question of ethics. . . . You can't compromise your standards."

When you decide that there are some ethical standards that are absolute, that you will never violate these standards regardless of the consequences, it transforms the way you make your choices. In your mind, you make a preemptive determination not to consider taking the unethical course of action. Then everything becomes simpler. There is no wrestling with temptation, no weighing of the risks, no cost-benefits analyses of the low road versus the high road. You do the right thing because you already have identified it as the *only* option. That is why ethical behavior has an almost automatic quality to it. It becomes as natural as breathing or jumping out of the way of an oncoming truck, as one leader said. People who orient this way to moral choices are in an enviable position. They experience a great peace of mind as they respond to life's events, and they acquire a well-deserved reputation for integrity and dependability. They can focus their mental energies on coming up with bold solutions to intransigent problems, because they are saved the debilitating equivocation on moral choices that plague people with less stable ethical compasses.

Ethics and the Purposeful Life

The only way to arrive at a firm ethical commitment of this kind is to see the centrality of ethics to the life that you desire. Reflecting on your ideal self is an essential way of developing this vision. Reflecting on the deepest purpose of your work is another. In people with the steadiest ethical bearings, these two streams of reflection come together, creating a vivid sense for them of the standards that they must follow if they are to find success and satisfaction in their work.

Amy Francetic, who produces demonstration mobile events for IDG Executive Forums, part of a large publisher in Boston, discussed with us people who had been role models for her during the early phases of her career. Like many businesspeople, Francetic encountered individuals along the way who had a strong positive influence on her self-development; and she encountered others who were "anti-mentors." She modeled herself precisely on what these "anti-mentors" were *not* like, as she disrespected the poor ethical choices that they made. Francetic is convinced that unethical behavior is a recipe for personal failure, even if, somehow, one manages to

*Amy Francetic with
daughter Lucy*

get away with it in a financial sense. Speaking of her days at some large toy companies where she worked her way up the corporate ladder, Francetic said:

> There were a lot of folks that I just didn't like their ethics. They would clearly lie to people. They would say one thing to one group and then say something else to another group. From a business standpoint I felt that was really bad practice and would come back to bite you. Other people just treated people terribly. . . .
>
> I really think that comes back to get you. Some people get away with murder their whole lives, you know, and they're going to make a ton of money and they've cheated their way to the top or whatever they've done, and I just sort of feel that if it doesn't come back to you in business, then it comes back to you in your health, or it comes back to you in your relationships, or it comes back to you somehow, karmically, in some other way.
>
> So I've always felt like it's really important for me not to have a lot of regrets about how I managed my interactions with my coworkers as well as business partners on the outside. And that there was a certain amount of integrity. And if we didn't believe in what we were doing, then that was a real lesson too.

"Believing in what you are doing" is the thread that ties the whole bundle of your personal aspirations about self, work, and life together into an ethical frame. Almost all the business leaders we interviewed took this as the first principle of their career aspirations.

C. William Pollard

The meaning of their work was their true bottom line—not replacing financial gain, which they also saw as essential, but superseding it as a matter of ultimate concern. When you keep the moral purpose of your work firmly in mind, ethical conduct comes easily and naturally, with little need for agonizing doubt or equivocation.

One of the most striking findings of our study is this near unanimity of attention to the higher meaning of their work. For example, C. William Pollard, the chairman and CEO of ServiceMaster, has said: "For most people, the firm is all about maximizing profits. From my perspective, it cannot and should not be the sole purpose of the firm. When it is, I believe that it is ultimately self-destructive, because I do not think you can generate profits without people; if people do not have a purpose and meaning beyond generating profits, you will come up against the law of diminishing returns. In the long run, you are not going to have consistent production of quality products and services unless people see a mission beyond profit. People work for a cause, not just a living."[9]

In our interview with Pollard, he said that what brought meaning to his work was his goal of fostering the development of his employees. He told us: "So, as I've seen people grow as individuals, grow in who they're becoming as well as in what they're doing, grow as parents, grow as contributors in their community or contributors in their churches or places of worship, grow as healthy citizens, all those things are fulfilling to me and bring meaning to the fact that work results in that."

Norm Augustine

In a similar vein, Norm Augustine, the chairman and CEO of Lockheed Martin, said that "what I was trying to do was build the greatest aerospace company in the world, and I thought that if we did that, maybe that would increase shareholder value. But to me you have to have a more lofty goal than making money." From this conviction flowed Augustine's commitment to ethical behavior. Interestingly, in discussing ethical behavior with us, Augustine commented that "the Golden Rule is as good a summary as anything I can think of." He said that most of the businesspeople with whom he deals are "very decent, very ethical," and this is no accident.

Augustine related a story in his interview that directly speaks to the strong links between purpose and ethical choice. When launching a spacecraft, his company receives a large bonus from the customer if the spacecraft safely completed its mission. One day, an insurance company offered to insure such bonuses in case of mission failure. The insurance was priced cheaply, and it offered a win-win prospect for Augustine: "If the spacecraft blew up, we'd collect from the insurance company, and if it didn't blow up, we'd collect from the customer."

Augustine saw this as an ethical question. Even though the insurance might be in the best interest of his shareholders, it violated the customer's intent. After all, the customer was not offering a bonus simply to maximize Augustine's take-home profit. The customer offered the bonus as an incentive for a successful mission. "I always distinguish between short term and long term," he said, "because I think so many ethical cases are cases where in the short term, if you do the right thing, it hurts the bottom line. But I truly believe that if you can build a reputation as somebody [who] can be trusted, business opportunities will come to you for the long term that will more than make up for the penalties that you pay in the short term, by and large."

Augustine—himself an engineer—also sensed that the bonus incentive would be irrelevant to the workers in the factory and on the launch pad. They would do their best to build a high-quality spacecraft whether or not the company received a bonus. So it wasn't really needed as an incentive. This made the insurance idea even more palatable, however, because if the incentive wasn't needed, there was no reason to worry about the possibility that the insurance would weaken the incentive.

Still, in the end, Augustine decided that he was ethically required to deal with the customer in good faith by making sure that he was honoring the customer's intent. To see whether the customer cared about the insurance policy, Augustine went to the customer and informed him of the situation. "They said they cared a lot," he reported, "and so we didn't buy it." In this way, Augustine took his ethical cue from the customer's purpose in arranging the bonus, a purpose that he shared when he accepted the deal. Using that shared purpose as a moral touchstone, Augustine saw that his only honorable option was to disclose the new insurance offer to his customer so that he could make sure that his course of action was consistent with that purpose. When the customer replied that no, it wasn't, Augustine's ethical dilemma was immediately solved. The surest way to determine the right ethical choice is to recall your moral purpose and choose acts that are consistent with that purpose.

Legendary businessman Ted Turner, the founder of CNN, told us that he "never did anything dishonest in business, or unethical. I [have] always beat my opponents fair and square. I [have] always played by the rules, written or unwritten." Inextricably connected with this ethical stance was Turner's conviction that he do something crucially important for the world. He had the sense that many global conflicts arose from, or at least were aggravated by, a lack of good communication among the opposing parties. When he started

CNN, the United States and the Soviet Union were at loggerheads over a host of conflicts stemming from the disparate worldviews of communism and capitalism. (One of Turner's other responses to this problem was creating the Goodwill Games in the 1980s.)

Turner created the first truly international, twenty-four-hour news outlet, broadcast to every corner of the world. For the first time in human history, anyone with access to a television set could watch the same news unfold and obtain the same information about current events. Turner told us: "I thought it was going to be helpful to everybody. I was a Rotarian, so was my father, and their motto was, He who profits most serves the best. I have always felt that you profited better if you had a strong service component to what you are doing. I did that all the way through. . . . I always had a strong commitment and a high sense of social focus on what I was doing."

This refrain was echoed with such frequency in our interviews that it leaves little doubt about the sentiment's profundity and sincerity. One CEO of a large manufacturing company worried that the current ethical climate in business may represent a "bad cycle" in human history, and he identified the root cause as lack of a higher purpose on the part of aspiring businesspeople. He also located the problem in the failure of business schools to teach ethics in a way that inspires a sense of higher purpose. This CEO said: "Too many of these young people [with degrees from] . . . business schools, their major aim is to say, 'Well, I want to make a million dollars before I'm thirty.' They don't say, 'I want to do a good job or help build a company' or something like that. There's nothing much selfless in them, and they're doomed to failure if there isn't a high selfless quality in their own values." Like other business leaders celebrated in this book, this CEO believes that the ethical behavior that flows from a noble purpose not only serves humanity, it also enables personal success.

Ethics and Personal Growth

Real ethics cannot be understood as a disconnected set of rules. Ethical behavior is wholly embedded in a person's larger sense of self and society. What kind of a person do I want to be? How can I become that person? What do I want to accomplish in life? What do

I want to leave behind? In the answers to these questions, people find compelling reasons to act ethically.

When understood as a central component of a person's identity, instead of as a separate rule system externally forced on the person, ethics acquires a positive rather than constraining quality. It then becomes possible to see how strong ethics can help us achieve our loftiest goals. Ethical acts become part of the tool kit for solving life's problems and expanding personal frontiers. Along with affiliated character virtues such as honesty and humility, ethical acts keep us on course in the direction that best serves the long-term interests of everyone in the picture—ourselves, our companies, as well as society and the world at large.

The key to this understanding is to focus on the big questions—who I am and what I want to accomplish in the highest sense—even amid the most severe pressures of competition and crisis in everyday business life. This is easier said than done, however, but it is a capacity that can be cultivated over time, much like any useful skill or habit. Many business leaders acquire this capacity through religious or spiritual faith. In our study, for example, we found that a majority of the business leaders interviewed were people of devout faith, even though they often avoided expressing religious views in their workplaces. Faith is one way—not the only way, but a powerful one—to keep a steady ethical compass amid temptations and pressures to compromise.

McDonald Williams, the CEO and chairman of the board at Trammel Crow Company, the huge Dallas real-estate outfit, recalled the times in his life when he wondered whether he was going to make it economically. One instance was back in the early seventies, during a severe recession. He was still a young man then, with four children and a mortgage on his home. "I'm busted," he said, "and you talk about a moment of truth, but what came to me at that time was probably as close to an epiphany in business as I've ever had, and that is, 'Wait a minute, why did you come? You came here because of the people and the values. Had those things changed? No. External business environments have changed. We're in trouble, but the reasons I came persist, and I can make a difference in this environment.'" Williams survived the crisis of the early seventies and prospered, only to watch his company fall back into another economic downturn in the late eighties. He explained the role of his faith in keeping a steady grip on his sense of purpose and his ethical values during these difficult periods:

> Values get tested on tough times, not good times. And I think that my faith helped, because once I went through that first time, I said, "Wait a minute, I'm not my net worth. I'm not my business reputation." And I never lost sleep going through the hardest times. We had guys who weren't going to sleep and their marriages were breaking up and they were doing things that they shouldn't be doing. But I think faith for me gave me an internal perspective. . . .
>
> My faith was more relevant to my business in tough times than anything else because then your values really were square in your face. Are you going to live them or not? Are you going to look beyond the moment for a longer time frame? Who are you? Are you just your job? Are you just your career? Or are you just your reputation? Or are you just your net worth? . . . I mean, they are important to me, I can't deny that. But I think faith helped me, in that moment, have perspective.

Ethics and Faith

In a similar vein, Dickie Sykes, the assistant vice president and equal employment officer of AMEC Construction Management, integrates all her personal goals around her belief in the higher purpose of her vocation. For Sykes, this has the ultimate spiritual as well as personal significance: "I have a strong spiritual foundation, and this isn't for everyone. I don't think people should impose their beliefs on others, especially in the work environment. But I can say personally that having a strong conviction that everything is going to work out—number one, it keeps you calm; number two, it keeps you from being desperately afraid of the unknown, to the point where you're immobilized."

Sykes's purpose is to promote opportunity for all in the workplace, a purpose that is linked directly to the ethical standard of fair-

Dickie Sykes

ness: "What I'm trying to accomplish, basically, is to ensure that we have equity and fairness on all of our project sites and in our internal work environment, ensuring that minorities and women get treated fairly and equitably in the workforce. Also, to ensure that small, minority-[owned], and women-owned businesses get treated fairly in our construction projects across the country. All of it has worth and meaning. When someone comes up to you and says, 'Dickie, you helped put my children through college'—no amount of money gives you that feeling. It's indescribable to know that what you do changes people's lives."

Many people who succeed in business over the long haul have refused to compartmentalize their ethical and financial goals. They have a sense of wholeness in their approach to every aspect of their lives: indeed, this is the very meaning of the word *integrity*. The wholeness is made possible by their dedication to the higher purpose that defines what they are trying to accomplish and, ultimately, who they are and what kind of person they strive to be. As do Williams and Sykes, many businesspeople look to faith as a way of preserving their integrity when ethical challenges arise, although other leaders find secular beliefs to keep themselves ethically oriented.

Richard Jacobsen is a real-estate developer and property manager in Northern California. He is consciously aware of the intimate connections between his business goals and his determination to live an ethical life. A devout Mormon, Jacobsen is one of the many business leaders with whom we spoke who centers his multiple aspirations

Richard Jacobsen

around his religious faith. In his interview, he was highly articulate about the ways in which all of a person's motives—financial, moral, personal, and spiritual—must join together for true success.

Jacobsen's endorsement of a "whole person" approach to business is right in line with the message that we heard from almost all of the business leaders in our study: "I think it's really a whole, it's not one thing or another. It's the whole, sort of a holistic approach. You're not just well if you're physically well, but you're well if you're mentally well, emotionally well, physically well, and spiritually well. I'm successful if I'm successful in my business and in my home and in my community and in my church. All of those aspects have to be cultivated together. The measure of success is not one or the other but all of them taken together."

Ethics, Character, and Integrity

The essence of the whole person is character, for it is character that gives a person "wholeness," that is, integrity. Character is composed of such virtues as honesty, which points the way to the ethical standards that enable a person to live a moral life. As mentioned here and in previous chapters, honesty is a primary ethical standard for any person in business, as is a commitment to the Golden Rule, because these standards create the climate of trust required for lasting business relationships.

The other character virtue central to enduring success is humility. In his interview, Jacobsen articulated the connection between humility, strong ethical values, and lasting business success: "My experience in business—I mean, my partner says, 'Always sell short on arrogance.' We have guys show up in the conference room, and I mean it isn't a very fancy conference room, and they're wearing—they['ve] got the expensive briefcase and the Rolex watch and the gold chains around the neck, and they flew in on a Lear jet, and you just put them on the shelf and wait your time and you're going to see that they're going to go up in smoke. . . . The people that I've seen [who] have really lasted tend to just be built on strong values."

The connectedness of ethical values, character, and purpose argues for a fully integrated rather than a compartmentalized approach to business and life. For educators who would promote high ethical standards in the men and women who go into business, the message is clear: you must emphasize matters of ultimate concern that drive people's noblest purposes and define all our ethical values. For an enlightened vision of success, these will be moral concerns, aimed at service to the world as well as to the self.

For those who choose business as their career—or, more to the point, as their calling—the challenge is to sustain an ethical life amid constant pressures to compromise and sell out. If you see this as a new challenge every time a new pressure arises, you will be certain to fall short of your goal. The pressures are too relentless and the temptations too alluring. You must keep your eye on the ball. And what is the ball? It is, once again, the whole person, the kind of person that you want to be, considered in all its aspects, now and in the future. What kinds of relationships do you wish to have with the people in your life? What contributions do you hope to make to the world in your lifetime? What is the way you wish to be remembered, the part of you that you will leave behind? What is the true source of your deepest satisfaction, and how can you keep aiming at it over the long haul?

For many businesspeople, the quest begins with finding purpose in the work that they do and then achieving success in an honorable manner. But it does not end there. Once success is gained, many believe that is important to "give back" to the society that supported their work. More than 80 percent of the business leaders in our study said that they were heavily involved in philanthropic giving. Dickie Sykes, the construction company executive mentioned earlier, spoke for many when she summed up the links between her vision of the person she wants to be, her career aspirations, and her desire to "give back" through philanthropy: "I'm a philanthropist at heart. That's the core of who I am. When seeking out a career, for me personally, it was never about how much money I could make. I mean everyone wants to make a decent salary in life. Let's face it, you have to pay bills. But to me it has to be integrated with something that gives back to mankind, something that helps people . . . because that's who I am and that's what makes me feel good about who I am, just simply being a human being. So it fulfills my own internal philosophy on what I think should be done in society at large."

Philanthropy, like business, can be a noble enterprise. But—and this may come as a surprise—it also shares some of the moral hazards of business, despite its charitable intentions. Because so many people in business see philanthropy as the capstone to a moral business life, I have dedicated Chapter 6 to an examination of the opportunities and pitfalls of philanthropic giving.

6 Philanthropy in Business: Doing It Right

The essence of philanthropy is compassion. The word itself, in its ancient Greek semantic roots, means "love of humanity." For societies that are organized around private enterprise (and the United States is the most prominent example), philanthropy provides a bedrock of care for the needy as well as a pillar of support for such nonprofit organizations as educational and cultural institutions. People who dedicate their time and resources to philanthropy have good reason to believe that they are making crucial contributions to the well-being of their society.

The value of philanthropy is widely recognized throughout the business community. As I noted in Chapter 2, almost four-fifths (79 percent) of the men and women whom we interviewed reported engaging in philanthropic giving to a significant degree. Consistent with the theme of this book, they do not see their charitable activities as a sacrifice but rather as another way to achieve their highest career goals. These business leaders believe in compassion as a desirable end in itself; and they also see it as an effective and moral means toward their more worldly career aspirations. They see giving as beneficial for both the giver and the recipient.

Of course this is age-old wisdom, found in many religious and philosophical traditions, including the Bible. But it is by no means a relic of bygone times: today's successful business leaders are convinced of philanthropy's importance to their deepest moral and strategic goals.

Why Philanthropy Is Important for People in Business

The business leaders we interviewed gave three major reasons when asked why they engage in philanthropic giving. The reasons are complementary rather than being mutually exclusive of one another. Often these reasons were expressed as a piece, although sometimes one or another was given special emphasis or reflected a particular giving priority.

The first reason for philanthropic giving is a concern for the well-being of people in need. This is a direct expression of altruism, reflecting the compassionate spirit behind philanthropy in its purest sense. Most people dedicated to philanthropic causes over the long haul act, at least in part, out of concern for those in need. For example, McDonald Williams, the chairman of Trammel Crow Real Estate, does philanthropic work for minority students at a Texas university: "I'm on the board at Abilene Christian University, which is where both my wife and I went to undergraduate school, and we've been involved in trying to help get more scholarships for minorities, for minority faculty development, and to help the school address the issues of inner-city poverty."

The second reason for philanthropy is building community relations that will profit both the company and the local community. This is sometimes called *public relations*, a term that has acquired an unsavory connotation because it includes activities that are superficial and insincere. Yet when a public-relations effort reflects a genuine commitment to the public interest, it becomes a matter of enlightened self-interest that benefits everyone. Many of the business leaders we interviewed understood their own philanthropy in just this way. They saw no contradiction between helping their communities and furthering their business prospects. As one man noted, this is "right" as well as "smart": "One of our core values is giving back to the communities in which we do business. It started with our founder, who was poor, and he just felt that was the right thing to do and the smart thing to do."

The third reason for philanthropy is out of a sense of obligation to "give back" to society. For many successful businesspeople, this is seen as a matter of elementary reciprocity: their society has been good to them, endowing them with wealth, status, and opportunities to pursue and find their life dreams; now it is time to return the favor. These men and women are driven by their personal consciences. The obligation to give back is not just a responsibility to one's fellow citizens or society at large. Rather, it is a responsibility to oneself. As one CEO with whom we spoke put it: "We've been given great wealth; therefore we have a responsibility to give it away intelligently. . . . You can pass on a work discipline—it's important to work. But it's also important to give."

Each of these reasons—altruism, enlightened self-interest, and reciprocal obligation—is sufficient in itself to motivate a philanthropic act; yet most people in business are motivated by all three reasons. Among the people we interviewed, a clear majority explained their commitment to philanthropy as a mix of their concerns for society, their good business sense, and the dictates of their personal consciences. As noted throughout this book, mixed motives of this sort are the rule, not the exception, for worthy acts in the world. This combination of other-oriented and self-oriented concerns is realistic for ambitious people who want to be effective in every sphere; it also provides a way of sustaining a dedication to philanthropy without sacrificing their business interests. It is a motivational system with staying power.

The potent mix of altruism, enlightened self-interest, and reciprocal obligation that drives charitable giving has created a lively philanthropic scene in today's society. Organized private foundations spent about $17 trillion on public interest causes in the United States during 2003. Add to that the even larger amount of donations made by individuals on their own account, and it is clear that philanthropy plays a major role in shaping the public landscape. For the most part, this is a good thing. The cultural world—from art museums to libraries to institutions of learning—would be vastly barer; and the needy populations—from the sick and elderly to the economically disadvantaged—would be far more impoverished if it were not for the robust philanthropic impulse that flows from the business community.

Philanthropy: Not a Quick and Easy Way to Solve the World's Problems

Yet like many good things, philanthropy can turn out badly if not done in the right way. In fact, among those who cause the greatest damage to the world are the irresponsible do-gooders: one of the soundest maxims in the ancient store of wisdom is the paradox that "the road to Hell is paved with good intentions." It is even possible to do *more* harm than good with the wrong kinds of philanthropy—a bitter irony indeed for those who give generously of their time and money only to see their efforts wreak havoc among those they intended to help.

When businesspeople look to philanthropy for a solution to society's needs, as well as to their own compassionate impulses, they may find a rewarding experience that both benefits the world and provides them with personal satisfaction. Or they may find a frustrating, dissatisfying experience. What makes the difference in these two results? The difference lies in whether the person applies the same skill, care, and values to philanthropy that he or she has used to achieve success in the business world.

Too many people assume that simply being willing to give is enough to ensure a positive result. The reasons that move people in business to engage in philanthropic work can make them especially susceptible to well-intentioned errors that can damage the very cause to which they have dedicated themselves. The motives seem so pressing—the powerful combination noted earlier—that they rarely stop to ask the fundamental questions that they would ask of any new business venture: Who benefits from this investment? Who may be hurt? What are its unintended consequences? Are there better uses of these same funds?

The problem is that many businesspeople do not look beyond

the compelling reasons that they have for engaging in philanthropy. The reasons themselves are so well balanced—combining value to the self and value to society—that they seem to justify just about any act of philanthropic giving. Herein lies the danger. In fact, philanthropy is a serious enterprise, rife with pitfalls, risks, and other complications. Deciding to give philanthropically is only the first step in accomplishing good work. The reasons that bring business-people to that decision, however strong they may be, do not automatically ensure a successful charitable result.

It may surprise successful business leaders to hear that good work in philanthropy is at least as hard to do as good work in business. It requires at least the same degree of understanding, the same attention to moral means and moral ends, and the same kind of personal humility that provide the foundation for a successful business career. Just as there is a moral advantage in business, so too is there one in philanthropy. In fact, the ability to do good work in the two spheres is closely linked, drawing from the same source of character and virtue. It is true that everyone in business should engage in philanthropy; it is just as true that everyone should take the effort and acquire the skill to do it in the right way.

The first step is realizing that giving money away is not a surefire, straight-shot, slam-dunk means of doing good in the world. It is not a quick and easy way to solve the world's problems and promote your own interests by throwing money at your favorite social cause. In fact, philanthropy is a serious endeavor with the potential of doing great good or great harm, depending on how you go about it. Succeeding in giving money to good effect is every bit as challenging as succeeding in making money.

This statement is so counterintuitive that it requires some explanation. It is natural to assume that any act of charity is worthwhile and to feel good about any act of giving. It is hard to confront the possibility that some acts of giving can be harmful; and it is harder still to take responsibility for the consequences—and not just the intentions—of gifts. We tend to think that giving itself is such a laudatory action that this should be enough. But good work in philanthropy requires far more than the willingness to give alone.

The purpose of the following section is to provide people in business with the knowledge about philanthropy that they must have to do good work in this challenging endeavor. I focus here on the harms that philanthropy can cause, not because I believe that people in business should shy away from charitable giving—quite the opposite—but rather because I want them to understand that good work in philanthropy demands a humble attitude, a rigorous application of high standards, and a lot of careful and well-informed judgments.

Philanthropy Is an Intervention

As part of the same Good Work Project that has produced the examination of business leaders in this book, our team also has examined the leadership of people engaged in philanthropy at many of America's largest foundations (for the most part, a billion dollars or more in assets).[1] Our research team conducted in-depth interviews with people operating at the highest levels in these foundations: the donors who made their billions in business, board members, executive officers, and influential program officers. We also interviewed recipients of the foundations' largesse. The team asked about their experiences in philanthropy, their ambitions, their satisfactions, and their frustrations. The ultimate question is: what does it mean to do good work—as opposed to harmful and counterproductive work— in philanthropy? We wanted to know whether they are accomplishing the purposes that they imagined when they decided to do philanthropy in the first place.

This is a surprising question for those—probably most people—who assume that giving money away can only lead to good. In a similar vein, it strikes some medical students as odd that their profession's founding oath starts with the less-than-inspiring injunction "Do no harm." What a defensive way to begin thinking about a noble craft that relieves disease and suffering! Yet Hippocrates was conveying the point that all medical acts (other than telling a patient to do nothing) are *interventions,* and any intervention, no matter how benign and well intended, has the potential to change things for the good or for the ill.

Most medical interventions reflect benign intentions, however, although there have been some gruesome exceptions to this, such as medicine employed in exploitative experimentation, torture, or the harvesting of body parts. But malevolent practices aside, benign intentions can wreak havoc, especially when carried out with poor judgment, carelessness, rashness, ignorance, and arrogance. Hippocrates' injunction to "do no harm" long has served as a universal code of medicine because it offers physicians a needed cautionary warning, urging them to adopt a humble stance regarding the powers that they wield.

Unfortunately, philanthropic giving has no such universally recognized injunction to be careful or humble. Because philanthropy is a matter of giving money away, on its surface a wholly laudatory activity, there seems to be little reason to worry about possibilities of harm. How could a dose of money possibly hurt someone? Yet philanthropy too is an intervention, changing lives in ways that can be as unintended as they are powerful. Much like medicine, it generally is a well-intended intervention—although here too there can be exceptions, such as when people give money away for purposes of control, power, status, and personal glory. Whatever the intentions, however, these interventions can leave recipients in worse shape than before the money was granted. Andrew Carnegie, the legendary steel magnate who pioneered organized philanthropy in the United States, estimated that 95 percent of philanthropic dollars were "unwisely spent; so spent, indeed, as to produce the very evils which [the gift] proposes to mitigate or cure."[2]

Philanthropy's Darker Side: The Well-Intentioned Harm

In the earlier quotation, Carnegie was referring to the harm of supporting bad habits that sustain poverty. By now, this particular harm is recognized by most of the people and organizations that give significantly to charity. But other harms too can emanate from philanthropy (see Table 2)—some of them, to use Carnegie's metric, at least as grave as the problem that the gift was meant to solve.

Moreover, trends in philanthropy since the days of Carnegie and his wealthy peers (Ford, Rockefeller) have exacerbated this potential for harm. One such trend is the increasing bureaucratization of the foundations that the original donors set up. A self-sustaining bureaucracy can create careerist incentives for its staff, enticing them to depart from the important interests of the recipients that the foundation was meant to serve. Another trend is the emerging popularity of business and marketing models in the philanthropic world (sometimes called "venture philanthropy"), creating pressures that can distort, and in some cases directly interfere with, the missions of the grantees. I discuss these and other examples in detail below.

How well are philanthropy's possible harms taken into account by those who practice this worthy endeavor? Do practitioners of philanthropy ensure that their good intentions actually lead to constructive rather than destructive outcomes? Do they exercise the kind of caution, wisdom, and humility that Hippocrates urged on practitioners of medicine, that other domain of benign and lofty intentions? We have found many admirable standards of conduct among those who work in philanthropy. For example, there is a widely shared sense that those who dispense funds are "stewards" of the money that they control, and, accordingly, that they have a sense of responsibility to the public interest. There is an avowed respect for the grantees that they serve and a stated determination to act in a way that demonstrates this respect. There is a common belief in strategic thinking and planning, so that philanthropic funds may be used efficiently and to maximum effect. There is a widespread commitment to accountability, the honest assessment of grant-making results.

But when we spoke with grantees who received philanthropic funds, we found a huge gap between the perceptions of the philanthropists and the experiences of the recipients. Recipients rarely felt that they had been treated with respect; they felt that their efforts had been undermined by restrictions or requirements imposed on them as a condition of support; and they questioned both the priorities and strategies of the philanthropic world.

TABLE 2. Typology of Harms

Type of harm	Description	Example
Direct harms to lives	Harms done to persons, including but not limited to the recipients of the service provided by the philanthropy.	Medical trials on human subjects.
Weakening valuable nonprofit organizations	Harm done to nonprofit organizations and their personnel. Examples include pulling nonprofits away from their own missions and priorities toward the funding priorities of foundations; creating frustration in personnel regarding grant requirements (including length of grant cycles, reporting, and evaluation); inappropriate influence in the organization by the funder; provision of insufficient general operating support that negatively impacts the staffing and pay of the nonprofits and their personnel.	A medical research lab trying to raise money for exploratory work in diagnostic testing.
Disrupting real social improvement	Undue influence of people biased in their approaches to social improvement, with a tendency to be swept up in funding trends, and with little direct connection to the social problems and practices their resources are meant to address. This harm includes the crowding out of ideas that do not fit into the fashionable philanthropic trend of the moment.	The large-scale school reform efforts of the 1990s.

Destabilizing communities	Philanthropic bias toward social change whereby decisions are generally made by people removed from the problems they address, with harmful results to the communities that the philanthropy intends to serve. This harm includes fostering turf wars and competition between grant seekers.	The urban renewal of the 1950s and 1960s in which neighborhoods were replaced with the development of "projects."
Creating unhealthy dependencies	Unhealthy dependencies can be created in three constituencies: government (excessive devolution of responsibility); nonprofits (overreliance on single sources of funding); and recipients (reliance on unstable nonprofits).	Irrationalities in the welfare system, past and present.
Creating an underclass of nonprofits	Some nonprofits doing good work are less equipped to navigate the requirements of the funding world. They may lack the professional staff to draft sophisticated grant proposals and the personal connections to the foundation world necessary to successfully pursue funding.	Social clubs established in the 1970s by and for low-income recovering addicts.[3]
Subverting democratic principles	Undue influence on issues of public policy by a small and unrepresentative group that controls vast amounts of resources.	The eugenics movement of the early twentieth century.
Harm to the philanthropic endeavor	Certain practices can undermine the credibility of the field of philanthropy. For example, the existence of an exaggerated sense of what the philanthropic sector has the capacity to do, accompanied by a lack of transparency and accountability about what they actually do, can erode the public trust. Malfeasance and/or mishandling of philanthropic resources can do the same.	Prosecuted cases of fraud, abuse, corruption, and other misuses of donated funds.

The sense of disenchantment among these recipients surprised us, because we spoke only with highly successful grantees who have maintained long careers largely financed by generous support from the philanthropic organizations that they were now criticizing. Perhaps they could be accused of biting the hands that feed them, but (to switch food metaphors) they were not suffering from the taste of sour grapes. Are the hard feelings of recipients simply the resentment of people who don't like being forced to jump through hoops to garner support for their cherished causes? Or, as the people who are closest to the problems that philanthropists are trying to solve, is their discomfort a clue to shortcomings to which philanthropists should attend?

Although the perceptions of recipients may be distorted by their own personal trials in wresting needed support from philanthropists, their overall skepticism provides clues about the challenge of doing good work in philanthropy. Among other things, it suggests that doing good work may not be as straightforward as it first appears. It is clear that the happy act of giving money away is not always sufficient to win the gratitude of those who get it. Does that mean that the gift is also not always sufficient to improve their conditions in life? And, going even further down the skeptical path, could this beneficent act somehow *worsen* the conditions of those whom it is intended to help?

Indeed, the more I have examined this field, the more I have become convinced that, to do good work in philanthropy, it is necessary to begin with an awareness of potential harms and an understanding of how to handle them. Yet the problem of potential harms, beyond the most obvious misadventures, is rarely recognized and even more rarely discussed in philanthropy today. The problem of harm lies at the heart of philanthropy's greatest challenge: to ensure that changes inevitably brought about by the intervention of giving someone money will end up improving the conditions of individuals and communities. Until philanthropists take seriously the reality that any change can lead to unwelcome outcomes—and until it develops a systematic set of standards and methods to protect against this possibility—it will always flirt with irresponsible risks, hardly a hallmark of good work.

Types of Philanthropic Harm

Table 2 (pp. 134–35) identifies several types of harm that can result from philanthropic acts. Some of these are so obvious that they bring into question the common sense, and even the motivation, of any philanthropist who causes them. Other harms detailed here are more subtle, apparent only to those who worry about indirect and unintended consequences.

The philanthropists whom we interviewed were by no means oblivious to these sources of potential harm. Indeed, they identified most of the harms detailed in Table 2. But the recognition of potential harms was far from complete or consistent among the people with whom we spoke; rather, it was distributed scattershot among the group. All the philanthropists were concerned about particular negative outcomes that they themselves may have personally encountered, but they showed little awareness of any such outcomes of other philanthropy. Nor did they look for guidance to any third source, such as a domain-wide document analyzing the matter and setting out recommendations for dealing with it. Philanthropy, unlike most professions, has not produced for its practitioners a set of common codes, beyond the minimal requirements of the law, that mitigate or prevent adverse consequences that may result from philanthropic activities.

This is not merely an academic or hypothetical point. Even though the harms listed in Table 2 emanate from the propitious event of some person or institution coming into money, they can do as much damage as actions taken out of hostility. Consider the following examples, drawn from our interviews with both philanthropists and recipients.

Direct Harm to Lives.   The annals of philanthropy contain cases of egregious harm done to persons who have been used as means to such desired ends as medical and scientific research. One of our interviewees pointed to the deal with a philanthropist that Arctic explorer Rear Admiral Robert Peary felt forced to make after he left the Navy: "In order to fund his expedition, Peary went into the world of philanthropy. And he found a philanthropist who had achieved most of his money from the railroads in the late 1800s, and one of the things the philanthropist wanted was some human specimens of Eskimos for the higher purpose of research. So Peary went up to Greenland and he brought back six Greenland Eskimos, five of which died of pneumonia within the first three months of being in New York City."

In the course of the twentieth century, ethics codes, research boards, and legal sanctions arose to prevent this kind of blatant disregard for human life. Today's contemporary sensibilities reject the idea of endangering humans for the sake of research. But many argue that the temptation is still there, especially with disenfranchised and voiceless populations such as natives of distant lands, the mentally impaired, the critically ill, prisoners, infants, and the unborn. And tragic mistakes still do occur, such as in the case of Jesse Geisinger, a victim of experimental gene-therapy research. The risky procedure that led to Geisinger's death was administered by a university laboratory that had been funded by more than two dozen private and public philanthropic agencies. According to his family, Geisinger was not made aware of the dangers of the procedure to which he was subjected. Also in recent years, concerns about fatal results from well-intended research have been raised in connection with control trials for AIDS research and other high-profile, philanthropically supported scientific ventures.

Weakening Valuable Nonprofit Organizations.   It is strange to think that a nonprofit group that relies on charitable gifts could be somehow harmed by some of those gifts. Yet this can be one more instance of the bitter irony that Andrew Carnegie noted when he remarked that many gifts exacerbate the problem they were designed to solve. Like individuals, organizations can become overly dependent on charitable donations and can acquire unhealthy habits in the wake of this dependency.

The most prevalent—and corrosive—set of bad habits is acquired in the effort to keep the money spigot open. Often this requires not only salesmanship but also some modification of the organization's activities to match the donor's priorities. This is not always a bad thing: donors may have constructive ideas about projects and services that can help an organization meet its mission. But sometimes the donor's requests (or demands) can undermine the mission by inducing recipients to operate in ways that depart from their better judgment.

For example, an art museum or a library may have its hands full simply providing its basic services to the community that it serves. Everyone agrees that such services enrich the community in irreplaceable ways, yet the museum or library constantly struggles to meet its budget, and few donors are interested in providing mere survival funds. What they are interested in are splashy new programs that garner special acclaim and publicity. The temptation for staff is to launch programs as a way of chasing funds, even if this further saps their organization's infrastructure resources and diminishes its capacity to provide its essential services.

This temptation is exacerbated whenever an organization is required to go to multiple donors, all of which have their own idiosyncratic beliefs and priorities. Creating proposals to satisfy a multiplicity of diverse, and often contradictory, expectations can be an exercise in Rube Goldberg–style design. Consider, for example, the case of a medical research lab trying to raise money for exploratory work in diagnostic testing:

> We were able to secure an initial seed grant from NIH [the National Institutes of Health] and then a larger grant from a private foundation that required matching funds. That got us entangled in a long series of conversations with smaller foundations, family run, and then some wealthy individuals who were interested in this area. They all wanted their own proposal in language that addressed their issues, they all had conditions and suggestions about how to go about things, but none of them knew any more than any layman about medical research. One of them wanted us to start with a survey of what doctors would be likely to use given their time constraints and then build the design around that. Another said we should bring in scientists with different perspectives than ours to collaborate with, to make sure that we covered all the bases. They even had ideas about what to

look for, sampling issues, technical stuff that they must have got-
ten opinions about from the press. Most of the ideas were totally
unworkable, and the back and forth on it has been frustrating and
distracting and it continues to be to this day, even from the
groups who finally decided to fund us on the grounds that we laid
out. We're not sure that we won't get the rug pulled out from us
somewhere down the line for some arbitrary reason that will pop
into someone's head.[4]

The distractions here include expending time and resources on constant fund-raising and proposal writing, combating illegitimate pressures to adopt poorly conceived strategies, and living with the inse-
curity of not knowing when or why future funding may be cut off.
Such distractions can weaken recipients' capacities to pursue their
primary missions by blurring their focus and making long-term
planning impossible.

The "venture philanthropy" approach, guided by funding models drawn from business, is especially prone to confronting recipients
with debilitating distractions of this sort. Among the practices that
can undermine recipients' work are (1) positioning the philanthropist as a "partner" in the venture, with shared authority over operations, rather than as a more distant, hands-off investor, and (2)
expecting predictable results similar to quantifiable business outcomes from work on complex social, cultural, and scientific matters.
Trying to hold nonprofit organizations to such standards can be
worse than unrealistic: it can place at risk the uniquely valuable services that they provide to society.

Many in the "new philanthropy" school pride themselves on
their wish to start from scratch, ignoring the old practices and traditions that, they believe, will hinder the effectiveness of their
"investments." A determination to improve on past practices is
always laudable, but in most fields it is understood that this can be
accomplished only once the field's best practices have been understood and mastered. It is hard to imagine someone trying to become
a doctor by saying, "Oh, medicine is all wet, I am starting from
scratch." Yet that is what many venture philanthropists are in effect
saying, thus risking not only repeating the mistakes of their ances-

tors but also making new ones. But medicine has a solid domain as its touch point; and a certain level of understanding of that domain is required for certification to practice in the medical field. Because philanthropy has never developed its own domain, it has no way of recommending, let alone requiring, responsible practices to those who enter the field with no expertise or experience of their own.

Disrupting Real Social Improvement.   At any time in any society, there is a wide variety of efforts dedicated to improving the human condition. Some of these efforts are aimed at social change, others at preserving endangered features of the past. Some efforts are focused on developing fresh ideas through discovery and research, while others look at implementing ideas through new social and economic policies. Some efforts are local and community based, while still others are geared toward as broad a scale as can be imagined.

All such efforts are subject to market tests of one kind or another. A new idea must prove itself before it becomes persuasive. A social or economic policy must withstand assessments of its outcomes before it becomes widely adopted. In the natural course of events, contending ideas and policies attract advocates and compete with one another on the basis of their validity, utility, and efficiency. Social progress can be defined as the success of ideas and policies that lead to genuine improvements rather than those that lead to degradations. Societies that encourage unhindered generation, expression, and testing of innovative ideas are those most likely to enjoy perpetual improvement.

As a powerful intervention, philanthropy plays a role in determining which ideas and policies win out. Moreover, this role has increased exponentially in recent years, as the growth of philanthropic organizations and resources has created a philanthropic presence in almost every effort aimed at social improvement. On its face, there is nothing at all wrong with this: an essential characteristic of a free society is that any person and group has a right to play an active role in determining the direction of the society's future. But with every right comes a responsibility. It is a legitimate question—and one that pertains directly to our examination of good work—as to whether philanthropy is prepared to play its increasingly decisive role in a responsible manner.

From our interviews with executives and staff of large philanthropic organizations, four conclusions that speak to this question emerged:

1.　Contemporary philanthropy is biased toward goals of social change rather than goals of social preservation.

2.　Philanthropic decisions usually are made by people several steps removed from the problems they address and with little training in disciplines that study such problems.

3.　Philanthropic decisions rarely reflect the judgments of practitioners who have actual experience dealing with the problems addressed.

4.　Philanthropic decisions are heavily influenced by new trends that sweep the field with much enthusiasm and little skepticism, magnifying the effects of these sudden shifts in direction.

Moreover, both the biases and the limitations of training and experience seem to be largely invisible to many who deploy philanthropic resources. For those who are new to philanthropic giving, there is often little reflection about core assumptions or alternative ways of orienting to such basic issues as the wisdom of change versus preservation. Other philanthropists might not know enough to justify the move to application and the cessation of discovery.

As an example, in our interviews we found an unsolicited and unexpected consensus about one instance of this effect: the large-scale school reform efforts of the 1990s, which were experimental attempts to improve schooling through often massive injections of funds into school systems nationwide. When asked for examples of failures in philanthropy, more than three-fifths of our interviewees noted prominent initiatives of this sort, and none cited one of these efforts as a successful example. The reasons offered by our interviewees varied; some of them with a special interest in education made observations about principles of school change that are too technical to go into here. But there was agreement that funding patterns favored some approaches over others in arbitrary and unjustified ways, and the effects of these patterns were exacerbated by a group-think mentality that led most major foundations to support the same small circle of highly promoted initiatives. As for assessment, in most cases it was impossible to determine exactly what had happened because of poor documentation; and in the few cases where such identification could be made, the results were generally disappointing.[5]

The irony is that all this came at a time of lively experimentation in school reform, with much energetic competition among distinct approaches. At best, it is clear that the foundation-supported efforts contributed little to this fertile movement. At worst, it can be claimed that these efforts soaked up human and capital resources (there are only so many educators and school settings to go around, and when they become committed to one initiative, they become unavailable to others); that they crowded out more promising but less visible approaches that had not yet gathered the necessary momentum to sustain attention in the face of the more publicized initiatives; and that they resulted in a general discrediting of schooling improvement efforts.

I was fortunate to interview John Gardner, the visionary leader of America's nonprofit sector, shortly before his death. Gardner too worried about philanthropy's blindness to its own failures. He pointed to a belief system similar to the one I have discussed in this book: the sense that those who attempt good things need not concern themselves about the inadvertent consequences of their actions. Gardner, with his long history in the philanthropic world, knew better. He had seen much genuine social progress made possible by the generosity of charitable donors and the good work of philanthropic foundations, but he had also seen mistakes, setbacks, wrong turns, and serious harms caused by money incautiously given. "One of the problems with these things," he told me, "is that they go up and down, up and down." He went on to say: "There's something about lofty ideals that is at odds with clean-cut self-evaluation. You know, 'How can you criticize us when our ideals are so great?' That's why I like that cartoon from Peanuts of Charlie Brown on the pitcher's mound [watching the ball fly over the fence], saying, 'How can we lose when we're so sincere?'"

Those practicing such endeavors as medicine recognize that their efforts may result in harm as well as good, so they establish procedures and standards to minimize the possibility of harm. Although some practitioners of philanthropy take seriously the possibility that money-giving interventions may bring unsuspected harm, this recognition is distributed neither widely nor consistently across this diverse and growing field. Does philanthropy need accepted procedures and standards beyond the minimal legal codes that it is required to follow? Or should it be regulated less like a profession and more like a voluntary and pluralistic array of altruistic acts— diverse expressions of the charitable impulse that should always be welcome, no matter how they are done?

Unfortunately, these questions have not been resolved in philanthropy. The only codes of conduct that the field has examined are (1) a philanthropic act should reflect the donor's intent, (2) it must conform to legal requirements of the state, and (3) it should advance the public interest in some loosely defined manner. And even with respect to these principles, the agreement is often grudging, with foundation staff chafing under the donor-intent principle, donors often chafing under the legal restrictions, and everyone squabbling about what best serves the public interest.

Without shared norms that go beyond minimal legal requirements, it is impossible for any enterprise to reliably mitigate the potential harms it may cause. Most fields discover this case by case, after the fact, and respond by adopting a new norm. For example, patients are butchered by incompetent surgeons, so a new norm of medical training is established; a sexual scandal rocks a church, so a new norm of pastoral relations is endorsed; investors in the financial markets lose huge sums of money because of misleading information, so new norms of advising and accounting are put in place. Harm is not an acceptable risk, no matter how noble the intentions. Philanthropy shares with medicine and all other well-meaning interventions the imperative to take all imaginable precautions to prevent unintended harms that its actions may trigger.

How to Do Good Work in Philanthropy

Philanthropy is an essential part of a successful life in business, giving meaning and moral significance to the profits that you make and enhancing your reputation in the community in which you operate. The multiple reasons that make philanthropy a good idea have led to confusion about what "genuine" philanthropy is. Some people have incorrectly concluded that unless philanthropy is "pure" in its motives, driven by altruism alone, it is somehow contaminated by the donor's self-interest. If this were the standard, most of the great charitable acts of human history would be disqualified. In fact, as I have written many times in this book, all important moral actions are fueled by mixed motives, because life is complex and we relate to situations in many ways simultaneously. The surest way to do good in the world is to align your moral commitments with your self-interest, because then there will be no temptation to back away from the moral commitment.

The first principle for businesspeople is to begin with the realization that good philanthropy serves many worthwhile purposes— for society, the community, the company, and the self. These multiple ends make the philanthropic act more, not less, valuable. Search for giving opportunities that serve as many purposes as possible: these will be easier to sustain in the long run, which in turn will make the giving more effective.

The problem with philanthropy is not the purity of motives— that is a chimera—but rather the intellectual and emotional resources that you dedicate to the task. Real philanthropy is not a casual pursuit. It is a serious business, and I use that phrase advisedly. Indeed, philanthropy calls for much the same skill and attention as does business proper. This is where many philanthropists fail. Too often they think that their responsibility ends with the decision to part with some of their hard-earned money.

The second step, after determining that philanthropy is the right thing to do, is to realize that philanthropy is an intervention with the power to harm if not carried out properly. This realization is humbling, and it should lead to a cautious stance toward any act of charity. It is not easy to remain humble while giving money away: for one thing, people who want the money will flatter a philanthropist to no end if they think they have a prospect of getting some. But in philanthropy, as in business, humility is an essential virtue. It enables us to listen and to learn, to acknowledge mistakes and to correct them, and to remove our own egos from the choices that we make. The choices therefore will be wiser and safer. It is unlikely that a genuinely humble philanthropist will cause harm for long.

The third step is finding out about the complexities of the philanthropic cause that you wish to support, taking the effort to understand it on its own terms. Successful businesspeople often assume that what they have learned during their own careers can be applied everywhere else, and that any social problem can be solved through sound business principles. While this may be true in certain cases, it simply does not work in others. Problems such as encouraging creativity in the arts, fostering learning in schoolchildren, or preserving the quality of life in communities require a host of solutions that arise out of the particular issues related to these causes. Business principles may help, but they will not provide the whole answer. For constructive action, businesspeople must learn about the particular issues from those with experience in these domains.

It takes time to learn about a new domain, reflect on what you have learned, and then make a deliberate choice based on that reflection. Good work in philanthropy is not for the impatient. It is, however, a source of joy and meaning for those who invest not only the money but also the care to do it right. The learning that it requires adds a new dimension to your knowledge of the world, and the humility that it demands enhances your moral character. It is yet another pivotal instance of a moral advantage that yields personal satisfaction and growth for yourself and needed benefits for others in society.

7 Forging a Moral Identity in Business

There are two hazards in writing about morality. The first is that readers will dismiss it as marginal to their real-world concerns, an idealistic luxury that has little to do with our daily struggles for survival or fights for fame and glory. This hazard arises from a misunderstanding about what morality is and how it works in the real world. The aim of this book is to clear up this misunderstanding with a detailed explanation of how morality creates a valuable business advantage for those who employ it consistently and imaginatively. But the second hazard is less direct and harder to combat. It is that people who speak or write about morality have a way of sounding moralistic, preachy, and, worst of all, holier-than-thou.

It is essential that I take this second hazard head on at the outset of this chapter, not only because I do not wish to sound like a preachy prig, but also because being moralistic (as opposed to being moral) is antithetical to the message that I wish to convey. Being consistently moral is a matter of virtue, and humility is one of the primary virtues, in business as well as in life in general. People who are moralistic tend to be arrogant rather than humble, and their sense of superiority can lead their judgments and their choices astray. It also prevents them from learning from their mistakes—and everyone makes mistakes.

Morality is always a work-in-progress. People who remain aware of their own imperfections and determined to improve throughout their entire careers are the ones most likely to do the right thing for themselves and their companies.

Misdirections of a Personal Kind

I do not in any way feel "above" those who have been excoriated for making infamous moral mistakes in business. Rather, I believe that anyone can make such a mistake and, more important, that anyone can learn from that mistake and do better next time. Below is the story of my own first business venture.

When I was in high school, I wrote for a school literary magazine. In those days (to date myself), a town printing shop set the type for these magazines, and I had great fun working with the printers on layout designs for my stories. Indeed, I felt like I had acquired a magical new power to create professional-looking print products (this was long before the days of personal computers and software print shops). One day an entrepreneurial question flashed through my brain: *What kinds of print products did I and my friends most need?* The answer that occurred to me, unfortunately, was not school literary magazines. It was, rather, phony ID cards, to be used for the sole purpose of buying six-packs of the cheapest beer we could find.

So the business plan was as follows: I got the local printers to reproduce small cards that read "State of Wyoming Operator's Licence" at a cost of $25 for five hundred cards. (I neglected to note what was being operated and I misspelled *license*.) I then sold the cards at school for $1 per, netting a profit of $475. What ensued was not pretty.

One of my friends was caught using his fake ID at a liquor store in his hometown. He reported where he got the thing, and I ended up on "social probation" for the rest of the year. As part of my torment, I received stern lectures from two police officers—a "bad cop," who told me that if he had his way I would be "sent up the river" as a juvenile delinquent for what I did, and a "good cop," who patiently explained to me that I could have brought about terrible harm, such as causing a deadly drunk-driving accident. I also received stern warnings from every teacher and assistant principal in sight.

Looking back, there is no doubt in my mind that I learned a lasting lesson from my misdeed and its unpleasant consequences. My moral mistake was that there was no useful purpose behind my business venture. The business idea was corrupt from the start, accomplishing nothing more than exploiting a market demand that itself was illegitimate: the drinking-age law was on the books for perfectly good reasons, including the very real risk that underage drinkers could injure themselves and others in a drunk-driving accident. The only goal that I could have possibly had was making a quick buck by exploiting the scarcity of ways that my friends could employ to buy liquor, a scarcity that was, in fact, socially desirable. This hardly gave my venture a noble purpose, by any definition of the phrase.

Although at the time I was far from happy about getting caught, I was fortunate to receive such a stinging lesson while still young. The distinguished psychologist Fritz Oser has found that people learn many of their most memorable moral lessons from mistakes that they have made. Oser calls this the process of "negative morality."[1] In the course of development, we turn away from behavior that we discover to be wrong, abhorrent, or harmful to ourselves and others. We are lucky when we learn such lessons early in life, for a number of reasons. For one thing, mistakes made when we are young are more easily forgiven than those made when we are older. If the lesson is well learned, it helps us avoid further mistakes. And events encountered during youth are memorable and leave a strong impact on one's developing sense of morality.

But it is never too late for people to change their behavior after an experience of negative morality. Nor is it always necessary for us to experience the negative example firsthand. In our interviews for this book, for example, the majority of business leaders with whom we spoke referred to "anti-mentors" who demonstrated ways of doing business that the leaders did not want to emulate. Often the influence of the anti-mentor was as great or greater than those who were positive role models. In a few cases, the leaders gave the anti-mentors more credit for (inadvertently) helping them shape their values than any positive mentors they could think of: the moral misdirections were so sharp, and the consequences of the misdirected behavior so clear, that the future leaders felt compelled to build their careers around key contrasts with the anti-mentor.

People can learn new values throughout their lives, gaining knowledge from observing the catastrophes that befall themselves and others. What is needed is a vivid sense that the observed behavior was wrong and a framework of understanding that defines the right direction for the future. Many people improve their behavior because they have learned from their mistakes (this is the educational benefit that Oser has called "negative morality"). My own moral mistake stemmed from a lack of noble purpose in my business venture—or, to put it more baldly, a purpose based on little more than avarice as well as a disregard for the legal and ethical consequences. It was a serious mistake, and I learned a lifelong lesson. It is up to others, of course, to determine whether my adult behavior has reflected that teenage lesson.

Everyone makes mistakes. What is decisive is how we respond to our own mistakes. Do we take responsibility for them, do we make restitution, do we examine and reflect on those mistakes, do we try to do better next time? Even the most profound corruption begins in small steps—a compromise made here, a corner cut there. Without noticing it, we can be well on our way to moral degradation before anything has gone wrong; in fact, the first few steps down (*degradation* literally means "stepping down") may feel comfortable, even exhilarating. But it is never too late to stop and step back up. The prerequisite, of course, lies in recognizing the moral mistake.

Misdirections on a Broader Scale

My own experience provides a clear case of a mistake of purpose. Another type of purposeless business is a company set up to do only sham transactions. A so-called Ponzi scheme, named after the 1920s swindler Charles Ponzi, pays a return to early investors out of money collected from later investors, until eventually the pool of potential clients dries up and the whole thing collapses. Contemporary pyramid schemes work in much the same way, like a temporarily lucrative chain letter. Such dealings may seem like the stuff of sitcoms or B movies, bait for suckers but hardly a threat to serious-minded investors—unless, that is, major banks and pension funds all over the world are considered to be less-than-serious investors. Imagine the surprise of these sophisticated investors when some of the largest holdings in their portfolios admitted that portions of their earnings came from sham transactions with no more solid purpose than Mr. Ponzi's fancy charade.

It works this way: A trading company sets up round-trip trades for the sole purpose of booking revenues. Nothing is sent to anyone, nothing is actually received for the deal. The only consequence of the trade is an increase in activity and cash flow that the company can report to investors and lenders, creating the appearance of rapid growth. This is a "take the money and run" way of doing business. Rather than working to contribute something of value to its customers, the company's efforts focus on raising its share price. Some in the know may be able to grab quick profits before the artificial growth is discovered, but most investors lose out in the end. Meanwhile, customers end up paying higher costs, because the sham trades cause expenses that must be passed on. It is hard to imagine a business plan with a less elevated purpose.

As one of the trading companies that got entangled in such a deal was imploding, its CEO noted that the company's business plan and financial statements were "opaque and difficult to understand."[2] It is not known whether this CEO was aware of any deception hidden in these "opaque" statements, but complexity itself, whether intended or inadvertent, can be a way of hiding the truth and confusing observers. It also can confuse those who run the companies themselves. This confusion adds to the loss of coherent purpose essential for every worker in every company. It reminds me of a line from a Raymond Chandler screenplay, voiced by one of his hard-bitten characters: "Don't let yourself get too complicated, Eddie. When a man gets too complicated, he gets unhappy, and if he stays that way, he loses his sense of direction."[3]

Accounting firms have their own problems of purpose regarding their complicity in these schemes, both past and present. Historically, they have been the "enablers" that provided the financial support and counsel essential to the pursuit of these phony trades. Certainly the firms had some knowledge about what was going on, and certainly someone in these organizations must have realized that such deals have little to do with the reasons why banks and accounting firms exist in the first place. Did the founders of these firms have nothing more of a purpose in mind than to help clients avoid taxes and deceive investors and customers?

Accounting, in particular, has a proud tradition as a profession dedicated to establishing truthful accounts of complex financial matters. Arthur Andersen himself was a pioneer in finding ways to give the public open and "transparent" reports of obscure bookkeeping matters that some companies would prefer to hide. He did not allow his firm to act as a hired gun or company shill, but rather Andersen insisted that it serve the public interest and adhere rigorously to ethical standards. This, in fact, is how accounting became a respected profession: it kept its mission of truth-telling in mind even while selling its services. The original, and still valid, assumption of the profession was that, in the long run, truthful reports best served both the public interest and the company interest.

But the profession has lost its way in recent years. In too many cases, its leaders have seen their jobs as merely maximizing profits by letting clients get away with anything they can squeeze under the lowest legal barrier. One former Andersen partner, Barbara Toffler, protested her firm's negligence of its profession's true purpose: "All that was ever reported [at a partner's meeting] . . . in terms of success was dollars. Quality wasn't discussed. Content wasn't discussed. Everything was measured in terms of the buck."[4] Money, as I have written from the outset, is necessary for business success but it is not sufficient. By losing sight of the purpose of their enterprise—in this case, the accounting profession's important contribution to an honest reckoning of financial transactions—the accountants let the true value of what they were doing slip away.

When, inevitably, this short-sighted approach finally led to scandal, public outrage, the collapse of the Arthur Andersen firm, and the implementation of new legal restrictions on other firms, many leaders blamed everyone but themselves: the media were at fault for producing sensational stories that worried investors, lawmakers were at fault for not preventing the shady activities through better laws, and so on. Commenting on Andersen's demise, one industry expert noted that Andersen's CEO "never said he took full responsibility for this. That was the problem with everyone at Arthur Andersen. They are all so arrogant that none of them wants to take responsibility."[5]

Honesty and humility are the two prime business virtues, and both seem to have been sorely lacking in many of the accounting debacle's key players. But the more fundamental problem was the lack of moral purpose in the activities that got them all into trouble. The spurious trades were not about getting energy to people, the banks' loans were not about helping a real enterprise grow, and the accountants' analyses were not about revealing the real financial status of the companies that they audited. In fact, in each of these cases, the purposeless transactions interfered with the necessary work that these outfits were chartered to do. Not only were the bogus activities without noble purpose, they also diminished the capacities of important organizations to provide the valuable goods and services that their customers wanted to purchase. Apart from the dispiriting nature of such misdirected efforts, this is surely no way for a company to grow and prosper.

Industry after industry has drifted into this false path in recent years, only to discover that the way leads to rags rather than riches. To cite one other highly visible example, the music entertainment industry has been disappointed to see its profits decline precipitously in recent years, despite the clear demand for its products by consumers of all ages.

The answer, according to one trenchant analysis in the *Economist,* is that the industry's chieftains have neglected their core purpose, in particular the creative work (or "content") that consumers wish to purchase: "Perhaps the deepest explanation of the industry's woes," concludes the article, "and one where the media moguls are the most to blame, is that it has been distracted from its core com-

petence of manufacturing something that people will pay for. Amid
dizzying talk of convergence, so much talk (and cash) was devoted
to securing and developing new forms of distribution that the critical importance of content has been neglected . . . ; instant commercial returns were favored over long-term investment in creativity."[6]
Like people, industries that lose sight of their true purposes risk
becoming empty shells.

Much has been made in recent years of corporate fraud, corruption in the executive suite, and other abuses of trust by those in
managerial roles. Although the revelation of scandals is always a
healthy act, necessary for cleansing the system and discouraging further abuses, there is often a cartoonlike quality to the revelations.
Politicians and the mass media, in particular, have ways of reducing
such revelations to oversimplified stories of good versus evil. In such
accounts, the corporate world is made up of good guys and villains;
politicians tend to say mostly good guys and a few villains, and the
media say just the opposite. The damage, in either account, is done
by the villains (be they few or many), and so the cure must be to
expel the villains and let the good guys take over. But such simplis-
tic accounts diminish people's understanding of what goes wrong
and hamper the efforts to avoid similar problems in the future.

In truth, there is no Great Wall between the saints and sinners
of the business world. All persons in business are subject to constant
temptations to cut corners, bend the rules, and feather their own
nests at the expense of their clients and companies. Some people
hardly ever give in to these temptations, while others do so occa-
sionally, in small ways; still others do so regularly, as a matter of
course, and a few people actively pursue every scam they think
they can get away with. These are different responses to the same
desire—the urge that everyone feels to promote his or her own self-
interest. The differences in response do matter—in fact, they are *all*
that matter in the end—but they are distinct shades of gray rather
than separate colors of the rainbow.

Throughout their careers, corporate heroes and corporate villains have faced similar choices and have been lured by the same
rewards of riches and power. In some cases, both the heroes and the
villains even may have made similar moral mistakes early in their

careers. But at some point their stories part. Those leaders who go on to serve themselves and their businesses well learn from their mistakes and find ways to avoid illegitimate temptations—perhaps not 100 percent of the time but often enough to preserve their honor and their reputations. Those leaders who end up as targets of investigative reporters and congressional hearings have failed to recognize the direction that their self-serving behavior is taking them. Small acts of corruption grow into bolder ones, a corner cut here metamorphoses into a law blatantly ignored there, and almost without awareness, ambition has turned into criminality. "Time wounds all heels," as humorist Dorothy Parker once remarked.

In Pursuit of Moral Identity

No one begins—or ends—a business career as a pure saint or sinner. There is a great deal of continuity between those who commit the most egregious acts of corruption and those who shine as models of integrity. But there is one crucial difference: at some point in their careers, probably sooner rather than later, those who were destined to become examples of integrity stopped the corruption train dead in its tracks. They come to terms with their own baser desires. They honestly admit their mistakes when they make them and take responsibility for these mistakes. These business leaders decide that they will aim for a higher purpose, that they will take a higher road in getting there. They think hard about the kind of person they want to be, the face they want to look at in the mirror each day, the legacy that they wish to leave behind when they have finished their life's work. In short, these people forge for themselves a moral identity that defines their character in honorable ways and points the direction to careers that are rewarding in multiple ways—personally, financially, socially, spiritually.

How to Forge a Moral Identity in Business: A Ten-Point Approach

Anyone can forge a moral identity in business, but how? In this book, I have drawn key lessons from men and women who have successfully forged such identities. I end this book with ten principles that I have gleaned from their stellar business careers:

1. *Find a larger purpose that inspires your work.* People who are truly successful in business strive to "make a difference," to leave the world a better place by virtue of their career accomplishments. This does not mean that they neglect the moneymaking side of their business pursuits—far from it—but rather that they are always mindful of what these pursuits contribute to the world.

2. *It is never too early to find a noble purpose in your business career— and it is never too late.* Successful businesspeople find noble purposes at many phases of their careers, and in many ways. Some discover it by learning lessons of "negative morality" from their early mistakes, There is no single right road to a business career of purpose. There are many roads. The way that works for you is the right way.

3. *The path to success in business begins with an act of self-discovery.* Getting in touch with *all* your motives and desires, from the mundane to the spiritual, will help you figure out how to pursue them all without compromise during those high-pressure times when it may become tempting to let your most noble aspirations go. Once you discover the core goals that define the kind of life you most want to live and the kind of person you most want to be, you will have found a moral compass that can keep you steadily on target as you move forward in your career.

4. *Find mentors who represent models of success and integrity.* By observing a successful businessperson, you can learn about how to pursue the kind of career that will give you the most personal satisfaction. One excellent way to do this is to develop an apprentice-like relationship with someone whom you admire, who can show you what a moral identity in business looks like in the flesh and blood. The best leaders in the business world see such mentoring as part of the service for which they should use their positions of authority. Seek out such leaders—they will welcome the chance to advance your career with this kind of moral mentoring.

5. *Use your moral imagination to generate creative business solutions.* Many of the best ideas for new products and services come out of a quest to fulfill a moral purpose. Similarly, the best managerial solutions to tough personnel problems can be found through applications of your moral sense. A sensitivity to what consumers need, and a determination to respond effectively to that need, inspires winning entrepreneurial concepts. A commitment to a caring and ethical manner of doing business inspires inventive approaches to organizing employees. Among all of our creative mental tools, the moral imagination has the greatest reach and staying power, because we will go to the mat for the things in which we deeply believe. Successful new business concepts often require this kind of staying power, because without a sustaining sense of purpose, the early results from any new idea often can be discouraging.

6. *Use your moral imagination to transport yourself into the thoughts and feelings of everyone in your business world.* These include partners, employers and employees, customers, investors, and other community members. The empathy that results from this act of imaginative role-taking grants you the capacity to deal with these people in a productive and problem-free manner. It enables you to conduct your business relations according to the principle of the Golden Rule, treating others as you would like to be treated. This is a proven formula for enduring career success.

7. *Stay humble, especially after gaining financial power and influence over others.* When success turns into arrogance, we often lose our capacity to learn from our mistakes—or even to notice when we are making mistakes. Pridefulness harms everyone, and ultimately it can destroy the very purpose that has fueled our accomplishments. The only way to avoid this constant danger is to keep a healthy and balanced perspective on ourselves. Ironically, this can be hardest to do when performing the purest of charitable acts, giving money away through philanthropy. Many businessmen and -women who have turned to philanthropy fail the most basic test of doing more good than harm with their charitable gifts. The rules for succeeding in philan-

thropy are the same as those for succeeding in any business: keep a clear focus on your overall purpose, conduct all your relationships in an honorable manner, and retain your humility even as everyone is hanging on your every word.

8. *Find and sustain your ethical bearings by paying attention to both the ends that you seek and the means by which you seek them.* There are three questions that you should ask in your pursuit of any business goal: *what* am I trying to achieve, *why* am I trying to achieve it, and *how* am I going about it? Ethics will flow naturally, without special efforts, when you find clear and honorable answers to all three questions. These answers will be the best protection against the hazards to reputation and career that often come from the temptations to compromise that are ever-present in the business world. The integrity of character resulting from a wholehearted ethical commitment of this kind is an invaluable reward in itself, one that leads to great personal satisfaction.

9. *Resist the cynicism and discouragement that may arise with the realization of how far from perfect you really are.* We all operate with a mix of motives, and a moral life is found in the constant effort to do your best, and rarely in a pursuit of absolute altruistic purity. Anyone who expects perfection in this life is bound to become disappointed—including perfection from ourselves. We are obligated to do our best—indeed, it is in our own long-term interests to do so—but keep in mind that we are only human. We must set our expectations accordingly, so that we can avert the disillusionment that comes from an inflated sense of who we are and what we will be able to accomplish.

10. *When you attain a leadership position, consider it a service rather than a privilege, and use it to pass your purpose on to others.* In particular, find positive ways to influence the younger employees. Set up apprenticeships. Get young people engaged in the noble causes that inspire you. Mentor them in the same way that you have been mentored by the exemplars whom you have admired (see number 4 above). Young people need role models who can show them how to find their "callings" in their work. When you pass a noble purpose on to a younger generation, you place the

purpose in the hands of people who can pursue it with new talents, fresh energies, and their own innovative visions. This is bound to bring the purpose closer to realization than anything you could have done on your own. It is your gift to the young, a way of helping the next generation find the meaning that you have sought, cultivated, and treasured in your own life.

Notes

Preface

1. M. Csikszentmihalyi, *Good Business: Leadership, Flow, and the Making of Meaning*, New York: Basic Books, 2003.

2. H. Gardner, *Changing Minds: The Art and Science of Changing Our Own and Other People's Minds*, Cambridge, Mass.: Harvard Business School Press, 2004.

3. W. Damon, *Noble Purpose: The Joy of Living a Meaningful Life*, Radnor, Penn.: Templeton Foundation Press, 2003; W. Damon, *The Moral Child: Nurturing Children's Natural Moral Growth*, New York: Free Press, 1990.

4. H. Gardner, M. Csikszentmihalyi, and W. Damon, *Good Work: When Excellence and Ethics Meet*, New York: Basic Books, 2001.

Introduction

1. We administered a semistructured interview that questioned participants about their goals, values, influences, career and life histories, and views of the business world. The interview usually took about two or three hours, although there were a few that went longer or shorter. We told about half the participants that we were interviewing them because they had demonstrated high achievement and moral excellence

in their careers. For the other half, as a research control, we simply said
that we were interviewing them because of their high achievement. With
just one exception, there were no perceptible differences in the two sets
of interviews. (The one exception was that the group with whom we
used the word moral made somewhat more mention of their philanthropic contributions.) On the main issues covered in this book, the
two sets of interviews were essentially the same, so I have used them
together for the sake of my conclusions here.

2. A. Colby and W. Damon, *Some Do Care: Contemporary Lives of
Moral Commitment*, New York: Free Press, 1992.

3. Ibid.

4. There has been an enormous amount written about the relation
between morality and self-interest, some of which reduces one to the
other (Ayn Rand) and some of which sets the two apart in stark contrast
(Adam Smith). Often the terms are used idiosyncratically, so it is hard to
compare the different opinions on the matter. For the present purposes,
I am using the terms as one encounters them in the common vernacular,
to indicate either an orientation toward the good of others, the codes of
society and God (morality), or an orientation toward promoting one's
own narrow, moment-to-moment personal desires (self-interest). This
is a distinction that most people immediately recognize, despite its
philosophic/semantic shortcomings; and it is a distinction that makes
a marked difference in the capacity of any person's behavior to do good
or harm in the world.

5. For a historical account, see M. Novak, *Business as a Calling: Work
and the Examined Life*, New York: Free Press, 1996.

6. W. Damon, *The Moral Child: Nurturing Children's Natural Moral
Growth*, New York: Free Press, 1990.

7. W. Damon, J. Menon, and K. Bronk, "The Development of Purpose during Adolescence," *Journal of Applied Developmental Psychology* 3
(2002): 115–27.

8. H. Gardner, M. Csikszentmihalyi, and W. Damon, *Good Work:
When Excellence and Ethics Meet*, New York: Basic Books, 2001.

9. Colby and Damon, *Some Do Care*.

10. M. Seligman, *Authentic Happiness: Using the New Positive Psychology to Realize Your Potential for Lasting Fulfillment*, New York: Free Press,
2002; M. Csikszentmihalyi, *Finding Flow: The Psychology of Engagement
with Everyday Life*, New York: Basic Books, 2000.

11. Seligman, *Authentic Happiness*; Csikszentmihalyi, *Finding Flow*;

and R. Emmons, *The Psychology of Ultimate Concerns: Motivation and Spirituality in Personality*, New York: Guilford Press, 1999.

Chapter 1

1. M. DePree, *Leadership Is an Art*, New York: Dell, 1990.

2. R. Greenleaf, *Servant Leadership: A Journey into the Nature of Legitimate Power and Greatness*, New York: Paulist Press, 2002.

3. A. Colby and W. Damon, *Some Do Care: Contemporary Lives of Moral Commitment*, New York: Free Press, 1992.

4. Ibid., p. 29.

5. P. T. Barnum quoted in J. Mueller, "The Role of Business Virtue in Economic Development: Six Propositions Provoked in Part by P. T. Barnum," Templeton Foundation Institute for the Advanced Study of Freedom, 2000, p. 17.

6. Colby and Damon, *Some Do Care*.

7. H. Gardner, M. Csikszentmihalyi, and W. Damon, *Good Work: When Excellence and Ethics Meet*, New York: Basic Books, 2001.

8. J. Collins and J. Porras, *Built to Last: Successful Habits of Visionary Companies*, New York: Harper Business Essentials, 2002.

9. G. Gilder, *Wealth and Poverty*, New York: Bantam Books, 1982; M. Novak, *Business as a Calling: Work and the Examined Life*, New York: Free Press, 1996.

Chapter 2

1. Memorably, Balzac's biting quip was quoted to me by the head of a large New York publishing company when I first shopped around for an outlet for this book.

2. M. Medved, *Hollywood vs. America: Popular Culture and the War on Traditional Values*, New York: Free Press, 1993, p. 34.

3. E. Erikson, *Identity: Youth and Challenge*, New York: W. W. Norton, 1968.

4. M. Nisan, "Personal Identity and Education for the Desirable," *Journal of Moral Education* (1996): 25, no. 1, pp. 75–83.

5. A. Colby and W. Damon, *Some Do Care: Contemporary Lives of Moral Commitment*, New York: Free Press, 1992.

6. Ibid.

7. Ibid., p. 278.

8. H. Gardner, M. Csikszentmihalyi, and W. Damon, *Good Work: When Excellence and Ethics Meet*, New York: Basic Books, 2001.

9. W. Damon, *The Moral Child: Nurturing Children's Natural Growth*, New York: Free Press, 1990.

10. A. Etzioni, "When It Comes to Ethics, B-Schools Get an F," *Washington Post*, August 4, 2000, referring to a recent Aspen Institute study.

11. Ibid.

12. M. E. P. Seligman and M. Csikszentmihalyi, "Positive Psychology: An Introduction," *American Psychologist* (2000): 55, no. 1, pp. 5–14.

13. Ibid.

Chapter 3

1. W. Damon, "The Moral Development of Children," *Scientific American* (1999): 281, pp. 72–88.

2. Brenda Fink, personal correspondence.

3. M. Csikszentmihalyi, *Good Business*, New York: Basic Books, 2003.

4. *Dean and Provost*, March 2003, pp. 7–10.

Chapter 4

1. W. Damon, *The Moral Child: Nurturing Children's Natural Moral Growth*, New York: Free Press, 1990.

2. P. Ekman, *Emotions Revealed: Recognizing Faces and Feelings to Improve Communications and Emotional Life*, New York: Times Books, 2003.

3. Ibid.

4. Ibid.

Chapter 5

1. M. Novak, *Business as a Calling: Work and the Examined Life*, New York: Free Press, 1996.

2. Aspen Institute study, circa 2000.

3. A. Etzioni, "When It Comes to Ethics, B-Schools Get an F," *Washington Post*, August 4, 2002.

4. Ibid.

5. Ibid.

6. One exception to this is Michael Novak's fine book *Business as a Calling*, cited above. My comments on ethics in this chapter draw on Novak's learned philosophy. To my knowledge, his book has received far too little attention on the business education circuit.

7. Ibid.

8. Ibid., p. 107.

9. C. W. Pollard, quoted in *Religion and Liberty*, vol. 10, no. 3 (May–June 2000): 1–4.

Chapter 6

1. The Good Work Project consists of research teams at Stanford University (under my direction), Harvard University (under the direction of Howard Gardner), and the Claremont Graduate University (under the direction of Mihalyi Csikszentmihalyi). The philanthropy study has been supported in part by the William and Flora Hewlett Foundation and the Atlantic Philanthropies. For more information about the project, see www.goodworkproject.org.

2. A. Carnegie, "Wealth," *North American Review* 148 (1889): 653–64.

3. See W. Schambra's article "The Friendship Club and the Well-Springs of Civil Society," available on-line at www.schumachersociety.org/lec-sch.html.

4. Details of this story have been altered at the request of the recipient, but any nonprofit research center will recognize the general pattern.

5. See *Education Week*, October 21, 2000, for further details on the disappointing outcomes of the school reform movement as well as some rare exceptions.

Chapter 7

1. F. Oser, *Moralische Selbsbestimmung: Modelle Der Entwicklung und Erziehung im Wertebereich*, Berlin: Klett-Cotta, 2001.

2. *New York Times*, November 16, 2001, p. C1.

3. Raymond Chandler, *The Blue Dahlia*, Paramount Productions, 1946.

4. *Business Week*, August 12, 2002, pp. 55–56.

5. Arthur Bowman, founder of *Bowman's Accounting Report*, quoted in ibid., p. 54.

6. *Economist*, January 18–24, 2003, pp. 11–12.

Index

About the Author

William Damon is Professor of Education at Stanford University; Senior Fellow at the Hoover Institution on War, Revolution, and Peace; and Director of the Center on Adolescence at Stanford. Prior to coming to California, he was University Professor and Director of the Center for the Study of Human Development at Brown University in Providence, Rhode Island.

Damon has written widely on moral commitment at all stages of life. For the past seven years, Damon has been working on a collaborative project (with Howard Gardner and Mihaly Csikszentmihalyi) aimed at fostering excellence and social responsibility in key domains of contemporary work. The domains include business, journalism, the sciences, the arts, higher education, and philanthropy. As part of this broad "Good Work" project (www.goodworkproject.org), Damon has teamed up with a group of leading journalists (the Washington-based Committee for Concerned Journalists) to create a "traveling curriculum" in journalism studies (see www.journalism .org). This training program has already brought principles of good work to hundreds of print, broadcast, and Internet newsrooms.

Damon received his B.A. from Harvard and his Ph.D. in developmental psychology from the University of California at Berkeley. Between college and graduate school, Damon spent two years in New York City working with disadvantaged families and their children, an experience that convinced him of the enormous potential of all young people. Damon's research and writing in human development has been aimed at understanding how this potential can best be realized in childhood, adolescence, and adulthood.

Damon has received awards and grants from the John D. and Catherine T. MacArthur Foundation, the Pew Charitable Trusts, the Spencer Foundation, the Carnegie Corporation of New York, the New York Community Trust, the William and Flora Hewlett Foundation, the John Templeton Foundation, and the Atlantic Philanthropies. He has been elected to membership in the National Academy of Education. Damon is married with three children and travels widely for lecturing, recreation, and exploration.

Moral Capitalism
Reconciling Private Interest with the Public Good

Stephen Young

Moral Capitalism is a handbook to the Caux Round-table's code of corporate ethics—which has received attention around the world—showing readers how to manage market capitalism and globalization for economic and social justice and fairness and how to improve outcomes for people and societies from market capitalism and globalization.

Hardcover, 250 pages • ISBN 1-57675-257-7 • Item #52577 $29.95

The Highest Goal
The Secret That Sustains You in Every Moment

Michael L. Ray

The Highest Goal brings the secret and discoveries of the famed Stanford Business School creativity course to people who hunger for the highest way through this world, whether they are focusing on business or not. Ray shows that when your highest goal becomes a north star that guides you when everything is falling apart, a power source and larger context that keeps you going, even through the worst of times. Through a distinctive combination of practical analysis, spiritual motivation, and creativity, this book both inspires and provides practical applications that you can use every day.

Hardcover, 250 pages • ISBN 1-57675-286-0 • Item #52860 $24.95

Ideas Are Free
How the Idea Revolution Is Liberating People and Transforming Organizations

Alan G. Robinson and Dean M. Schroeder

Front-line employees see a great many problems and opportunities that their managers don't, but most organizations fail to tap into this extraordinary potential source of revenue-enhancing, savings-generating ideas. *Ideas Are Free* sets out a roadmap for totally integrating ideas and idea management into the way companies are structured and operate. Robinson and Schroeder show how to take advantage of this virtually free, perpetually renewing font of innovation.

Hardcover, 250 pages • ISBN 1-57675-282-8 • Item #52828 $24.95

Berrett-Koehler Publishers
PO Box 565, Williston, VT 05495-9900
Call toll-free! **800-929-2929** 7 am-9 pm EST

Or fax your order to 1-802-864-7626
For fastest service order online: **www.bkconnection.com**

Robert K. Greenleaf
A Life of Servant Leadership

Don M. Frick

This is the first biography of Robert K. Greenleaf, the pioneer of the philosophy of the widely influential servant leadership approach to management and author of Servant Leaderhip. Authorized by Greenleaf's surviving children, it is the story of the man who first lived the servant-leader philosophy, created the term, and applied it to management and organizations.

Hardcover, 300 pages • ISBN 1-57675-276-3 • Item #52763 $29.95

Managers Not MBAs
A Hard Look at the Soft Practice of Managing and Management Development

Henry Mintzberg

In this sweeping critique of how managers are educated and how, as a consequence, management is practiced, Henry Mintzberg offers thoughtful and controversial ideas for reforming both. He shows how the traditional MBA "trains the wrong people in the wrong ways with the wrong consequences." He calls for a more engaging approach to managing and a more reflective approach to management education, outlining how business schools can become true schools of management.

Hardcover, 400 Pages • ISBN 1-57675-275-5 • Item #52755 $27.95

The Peon Book
How to Manage Us

Dave Haynes

Written by an employee—not an "expert"—The Peon Book tells managers what they really need to do to make their employees motivated, committed, and productive. Haynes writes in a common sense, easy-to-read style that is both witty and wise. Every boss can benefit, and every employee can empathize with the words in The Peon Book.

Paperback original, 168 pages • ISBN 1-57675-285-2
Item #52852 $12.95

Berrett-Koehler Publishers
PO Box 565, Williston, VT 05495-9900
Call toll-free! **800-929-2929** 7 am-9 pm EST

Or fax your order to 1-802-864-7626
For fastest service order online: **www.bkconnection.com**

Berrett-Koehler books are available at quantity discounts for orders of 10 or more copies.

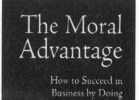

The Moral Advantage
How to Succeed in Business by Doing the Right Thing
William Damon

Hardcover
ISBN 1-57675-206-2
Item #52062 $24.95

To find out about discounts for orders of 10 or more copies for individuals, corporations, institutions, and organizations, please call us toll-free at (800) 929-2929.

To find out about our discount programs for resellers, please contact our Special Sales department at (415) 288-0260; Fax: (415) 362-2512. Or email us at bkpub@bkpub.com.

Subscribe to our free e-newsletter!
To find out about what's happening at Berrett-Koehler and to receive announcements of our new books, special offers, free excerpts, and much more, subscribe to our free monthly e-newsletter at www.bkconnection.com.

Berrett-Koehler Publishers
PO Box 565, Williston, VT 05495-9900
Call toll-free! **800-929-2929** 7 am-9 pm EST

Or fax your order to 1-802-864-7626
For fastest service order online: **www.bkconnection.com**